"This well-researched book is, t
Kenneth Langley takes the ge
lowing each facet to flash with
with new and exciting preach
new insight for psalm preachin

— **Thomas G. Long**, Bandy Professor Emeritus of Preaching, Candler School of Theology, Emory University, author of *Preaching and the Literary Forms of the Bible*

"Langley's work is a must-read for the preacher planning to expound a psalm or two (or a hundred and fifty). Chock-full of tips and strategies, all delivered to the reader in an amicable and avuncular tone, this tome will make you want to preach a psalm next Sunday! Take and read … and preach!"

— **Abraham Kuruvilla**, Senior Research Professor of Preaching and Pastoral Ministries, Dallas Theological Seminary, Dallas, TX

"In How to Preach the Psalms, Kenneth Langley gives today's preachers exactly what we need: fresh homiletical ideas on an important topic for our preaching ministries. We already sense how wide the gap is between the depth that is present in the Psalms and the shallowness that is present in our attempts to preach them. This book will not only help us close the gap; it will also challenge us to go wider and deeper as preachers."

— **Jared E. Alcántara**, Associate Professor of Preaching, Baylor's Truett Theological Seminary, author of The Practices of Christian Preaching

"For years I've used Ken Langley's various materials on the psalms in all my masters and doctoral courses. Now, pastors and students everywhere are fortunate to have his work in complete and published form. Ken has the depth and insight to write a book on preaching the psalms. In addition to being a scholar and teacher, he has been a preaching pastor for decades. In this book, he leads us through fourteen genre-sensitive strategies for preaching the psalms, showing how our sermons can capture, not only their meaning, but also their emotion. His footnotes, and 'For Further Study' citations at the end of each chapter, offer rich resources for anyone wanting to delve further into a topic. As you read through the book, you'll find yourself filing notes of Ken's discussions of various psalms, thinking, 'Whenever I preach this psalm, I'll want to read this page again!' This is a fine and helpful book!"

— **Don Sunukjian,** Professor of Preaching, Talbot School of Theology

How to Preach the Psalms

For Jennifer, who has heard me preach more than anyone and still loves me.

HOW TO PREACH THE PSALMS

KENNETH LANGLEY

Fontes

How to Preach the Psalms

FONTES PRESS
DALLAS, TX
www.fontespress.com

Contents

Series Introduction

The Bible is the best-selling book of all time. There are various reasons for that—it feeds us spiritually; gives us hope; points us to the Triune God; and shows us where we came from and where we are going. There's another reason: the Bible is great literature; just plain great. Captivating narratives, wry proverbs, dark prophecies, catalogues of laws, and practical but theologically deep epistles populate its pages.

However, the literary nature of the Bible creates a problem for preaching. What's a preacher to do with that fact that the Bible is literature? Are we supposed to create sermonic-poems when we preach psalms? Are we supposed to leave our meaning opaque when we preach certain parables? If the text is a story must the sermon be a story? What's a preacher to do?

One thing preachers could do, and have done, is to ignore the fact that the Bible is literature. Turn a deaf ear and blind eye to its literary qualities. Feed each text into the homiletical mill and crank out sermon after sermon as uniform as hotdogs. The authors of this series reject that option. Our conviction is that God inspired not only the content of the Bible, but also its forms. Cranking out homiletical hotdogs from quirky parables, awe-inspiring miracle stories, kaleidoscopic visions, and emotive lyric poetry violates authorial intention. Ronald Allen famously quipped: "To change the form of preaching to a form not clearly representative of the text is akin to covering the cathedral at Chartres with vinyl siding."[1]

---

1 Ronald J. Allen, "Shaping Sermons by the Language of the Text," in *Preaching Biblically,* ed. Don M. Wardlaw (Westminster, 1983), 30.

The authors share another conviction: preaching should be interesting. Holding an audience's attention is largely a matter of content—showing how the ancient Word applies to today's needs and interests—but it is also a matter of form. A steady diet of hotdogs is unappetizing.

So, how can preachers be biblical in form as well as content? That question is the impetus of this series called *Preaching Biblical Literature*. In trim and readable volumes, the reader will encounter methods and strategies for preaching the various genres of the Bible. We want to give preachers recipes for sermons that are as varied as the literature in the Bible itself.

Our goal is to provide succinct descriptions of these literary forms with concrete suggestions for preaching in genre-sensitive ways. Each volume is grounded in biblical and literary scholarship and applies those disciplines to homiletics. With plenty of examples in each chapter, as well as sample sermons at the end of each book, our hope is to teach and model how to preach biblical literature biblically. Here's to stamping out hotdogs. Let's get cooking.

Jeffrey D. Arthurs
Kenneth J. Langley

Author's Preface

Preachers need help with the psalms. Although scholarly and devotional literature on this longest book of the Bible comes out faster than anyone can keep up with, homiletical literature on the unique challenges posed by this part of God's Word is sadly lacking. Excellent commentaries are available. Exegetical, theological, and literary studies abound. But what use to make in the pulpit of all this scholarly insight we are left to figure out as best we can.

As Donald Macleod put it years ago, "The peculiar features of the Psalter as a piece of biblical literature take on homiletical significance because an adequate appreciation and understanding of these phenomena are prerequisite to any honest treatment of a psalm in a sermon."[1] *Prerequisite.* Once preachers appreciate and understand the phenomena of parallelism, chiasm, metaphor, deliberate ambiguity, canonical shape, and so on, we still have to decide how these poetic features will shape sermon content and delivery. Yet time and again, books or journals that appear to promise help on preaching psalms prove to be more about *interpreting* psalms.[2]

---

1 Donald Macleod, "Preaching from the Psalms," in *Biblical Preaching*, ed. James W. Cox (Westminster, 1983), 106.

2 Recent books by J. Clinton McCann and James C. Howell (*Preaching the Psalms* [Abingdon, 2001]), Dave Bland and David Fleer (*Performing the Psalms* [Chalice, 2005]), and James L. Mays (*Preaching and Teaching the Psalms* [Westminster John Knox, 2006]) illustrate what I'm talking about. From these titles, you might expect to find specific, practical counsel on how to move from the text in the study to the sermon in the pulpit. But what these authors and editors have, in fact, given readers, is insight into the spirituality, themes, theology, and

It seems to me that what preachers need is more of what Tom Long did in *Preaching and the Literary Forms of the Bible* (Fortress, 1989) and Jeffrey Arthurs did in *Preaching with Variety* (Kregel, 2007). Long steered preachers in the direction of genre-sensitive preaching "based on the relatively simple idea that the literary dynamics of a biblical text can and should be important factors in the preacher's navigation of the distance between text and sermon."[3] His chapter on Psalms is the seed from which the present book has grown (though my debt to Long's work does not mean he can be blamed for mine!). But Long devotes a single chapter to Psalms, when three or four book-length treatments are needed. Here's one.[4]

---

scholarship of the psalms—with *some* suggestive hints on how to let all this insight impact preaching. All three are, however, excellent books.

3 Thomas G. Long, *Preaching and the Literary Forms of the Bible* (Fortress, 1989), 11.

4 Homiletics classes will find useful discussion questions and assignment possibilities at the end of each chapter.

Introduction

*"What minister has not been captured
by a psalm, only to be defeated and hu-
miliated in his attempt to turn it into a
sermon? Poetry which soars, when treated in our halting words limps and stag-
gers along a dusty trail of dead prose."*[1]

Dwight Stevenson

For the first ten years or so of my pastoral ministry, I tended to
avoid preaching the Psalms. If anyone had asked why, I would
have been hard pressed for an answer. After all, the Psalms have
long been treasured by God's people, read and reread, sung and
prayed, memorized, cross-stitched, framed and mounted. They
touch hearts and fuel imaginations, they speak to every human
need, and do so in an aesthetically engaging manner—what more
could a preacher ask for in a text?

Yet I discovered that I was not alone in neglecting the Psalms. A
homiletical mentor admitted that he, too, avoided this part of the
Bible. Fellow pastors told me they felt the same way. "Best sermon"
collections rarely included samples on psalm texts. Walter Brueggemann confessed, "The Psalms are notoriously difficult preaching material."[2]

---

1 Dwight Stevenson, *In the Biblical Preacher's Workshop* (Abingdon,
1967), 159.

2 Walter Brueggemann, "Preaching as Reimagination," *Theology Today* 52,
no. 3 (1995): 326. See, too, page 9 in his contribution to a series of papers pre-
sented at the 2004 Rochester College Sermon Seminar, "Psalms in Narrative

Why? Could it be that the "poemness" of the psalms does not translate well into sermons? Maybe the very things that attract readers to these ancient prayers and songs make them hard for preachers? I was not sure, but I did know that on the rare occasion when I would venture to preach a psalm, I felt vaguely dissatisfied. What was vague then is clearer to me now: I had been faithful to the meaning of the Psalms, but their emotion, imagination, and aesthetic appeal never quite made it into the sermon. I had not captured the poetic essence of these texts.

I was almost prepared to agree with Donald Gowan that the psalms do not want to be preached, that they are speech directed toward God and do not adapt well to speech directed toward the church. So, Gowan said, we should pray the psalms and sing the psalms, but not preach them; use them for calls to worship and offertory sentences and benedictions, but not for sermons.[3]

But somehow this didn't seem right. If psalms are Scripture and if all Scripture is profitable for teaching (2 Timothy 3:17), then surely the psalms must be preachable.[4] Many psalms are intentionally didactic; indeed, one recent trend in Psalms studies has been to recognize their doctrinal and catechetical richness, their suitability as a source for instructing and forming the people of God.[5] All psalms, even those less obviously pedagogical, grow

---

Performance," in Dave Bland and David Fleer, eds., *Performing the Psalms* (Chalice, 2005), 1–30. McCann and Howell note other reasons the psalms are difficult preaching texts, including the fact that seminarians receive little instruction in the methodological tools that would help them preach the psalms (*Preaching the Psalms*, 15–17).

3 *Reclaiming the Old Testament for the Christian Pulpit* (John Knox, 1980), 146. Gowan's claim is especially striking in that it comes at the end of a book which pleads for more preaching from the Old Testament. He does modify his position somewhat by acknowledging that some psalms—wisdom psalms, for example—are addressed to human listeners and so may be considered suitable sermon texts.

4 Elizabeth Achtemeier insists that we not only *may* preach the Psalms, but because they are so important for growth in Christian maturity we *must* preach the Psalms: "Preaching from the Psalms," *Review and Expositor* 81:3 (Summer, 1984): 443.

5 See, for example, Gordon J. Wenham, *Psalms as Torah* (Baker, 2012); J. Clinton McCann, Jr., *A Theological Introduction to the Book of Psalms: The Psalms as Torah* (Abingdon, 1993); and the chapters by David G. Firth ("The Teaching of

out of theologically rich soil which can nourish the c
Thanksgiving psalms remind us of who God is and wha ..
for us. Laments remind us of God's compassionate heart and ou.
broken creatureliness. Royal psalms compel us to honor God's
kingship; hymns rehearse his justice and grace; Torah psalms
teach us to treasure his Word. Even an entrance liturgy like Psalm
24 can be read as a *credo,* full of theological affirmations. If this is
not grist for sermons, what is?

It is true that although the rest of the Bible speaks *to* us, the
psalms speak *for* us. But J. Clinton McCann warns us not to press
that distinction too far.[6] Their editorial arrangement and pres-
ervation in the canon bear witness to the judgment of previous
generations that these poems should be received as God's Word.
The Psalter is catechism as well as hymnal. Its compilers probably intended it to be received as Torah, its five "books" parallel-
ing the Pentateuch's. New Testament writers accepted the psalms
as instruction, often introducing citations with "God said," or its
equivalent. Between every line of these ageless poems lie doctrinal
claims about God and our relationship to him.

So Donald Gowan qualifies somewhat his exclusion of the
psalms as sermon texts. He admits that some psalm speech is directed towards people and is therefore, theoretically, preachable.
But he finds another argument against preaching the psalms—one
which may prove more compelling than the first, in practice if not
in theory: "The lyrical form of the psalms remains a challenge for
us ... unless preachers have special lyrical gifts of their own, how
can a sermon avoid sounding very pedestrian and dull in comparison with its text?"[7]

Many preachers have felt the force of this argument. We remember with embarrassment sucking the juice out of a psalm and
then preaching a shriveled rind of a sermon. We have read Warren
Wiersbe's indictment and know we must plead guilty as charged:

---

the Psalms") and Gordon J. Wenham ("The Ethics of the Psalms") in *Interpreting
the Psalms,* ed. David Firth and Philip S. Johnson (InterVarsity, 2005).

6 McCann, *Theological Introduction,* 73.

7 Donald Gowan, *Reclaiming the Old Testament for the Christian Pulpit*
(John Knox, 1980), 146.

In our attempt to be biblical preachers, we have so emphasized the analytical that we've forgotten the poetic. We see the trees waving their branches, but we hold the branches still, examine them scientifically, leaf and twig, and all the while fail to hear the trees clapping their hands to the glory of God.[8]

Some of us do hear the music but do not know how to sing it in the pulpit. Some of us find ourselves emotionally, imaginatively, and aesthetically captivated when reading psalms, but do not know how to captivate others when preaching them. As Gowan asked, "how can a sermon avoid sounding very pedestrian and dull in comparison with its text?" The following chapters try to answer this question.

For Further Study

Bland, Dave, and David Fleer. *Performing the Psalms.* Chalice, 2005.
Mays, James L. *Preaching and Teaching the Psalms.* Westminster John Knox, 2006.
McCann, J. Clinton, and James C. Howell, *Preaching the Psalms.* Abingdon, 2001.

Talk about It

How has your experience of preaching or hearing sermons on the psalms been like or different from Dwight Stevenson's, whose quote opens this chapter? What, in addition to their poetic shape, makes psalms (in Brueggemann's words) "difficult preaching material?"

Dig Deeper

Reflect on the title of Gordon Wenham's book, *Psalms as Torah* (if possible, read at least the introduction to the book). If psalms are meant as ethical instruction, what are the implications for their "preachability"?

---

8 Warren Wiersbe, *Preaching and Teaching with Imagination* (Victor, 1994), 35.

Practice

Listen to a sermon on a psalm. How, if at all, does the preacher manage to reflect the poetry of the text? Incorporate one of the preacher's "best practices" into your next sermon.

1

Genre

Saying what a poem means is quite different from breaking into poetry.[1]
John Stapleton

To change the form of preaching to a form not clearly representative of the text is akin to covering the cathedral at Chartres with vinyl siding.[2]
Ronald Allen

Compare these two lines:

"The LORD is my shepherd."

"God can be counted on to provide for his people because he is present and powerful."

A naïve reader might think that these two sentences mean the same thing in different words. But the naïve reader would be wrong. The second sentence paraphrases a line from Psalm 23 but loses something in translation—inevitably so, since meaning is not a matter of content only but of form as well. The aesthetic shape of the poetic

---

1 John Mason Stapleton, *Preaching in the Demonstration of the Spirit and Power* (Fortress, 1988), 59.

2 Ronald J. Allen, "Shaping Sermons by the Language of the Text," in *Preaching Biblically,* ed. Don M. Wardlaw (Westminster, 1983), 30.

line is not mere dressing; it contributes to and enhances meaning. Which is why one poet, when asked what his poem meant, simply recited the poem again. The meaning of the poem is the poem.[3]

Preachers know this. After years of reading different kinds of literature, we've learned to recognize different ways of meaning. We know that we cannot read a poem the same way we read an essay. We do not try to read hymns and grocery lists and train schedules and advertisements and limericks and love letters and novels and dictionaries and blogs all the same way. If we encounter words like, "Once upon a time," or "AP—Jerusalem," or "To Whom It May Concern," or "Batter my heart Three Person'd God" we recognize cues that what follows is to be read as fairy story, news report, business letter, and sonnet.

So, unlike our theoretical naïve reader, we do not expect a prose paraphrase to mean the same *in the same way* as a poetic line. We do not even expect different kinds of poems to mean the same: sonnets and ballads, haiku and limericks all work differently and are supposed to be read differently. We preachers, in other words, have developed a measure of genre-sensitivity.[4]

And most of us intuitively bring this genre sensitivity to our reading of Scripture. We do not read Proverbs the same way we read the Decalogue. We do not expect narrators to argue like the book of Hebrews, or Hebrews to tell a story like Ruth. We do not interpret apocalyptic the way we do Acts, or read psalms the way we read parables. When we encounter the words, "you shall not," or "the kingdom of God is like," or "the word of the Lord came to me," or "Paul, a servant of Jesus Christ," we recognize cues that what follows is to be read as legal material, parable, oracle, and epistle. And it's a good thing, too. We could never understand what God says in the Bible unless we had learned to read different kinds

---

3 Laurence Perrine distinguishes between a poem's "prose meaning," its paraphraseable content, and its "total meaning," of which form is a part (*Sound and Sense: An Introduction to Poetry*, 6th ed. [Harcourt, Brace, Jovanovich, 1982], 132). See also John Dewey, *Art as Experience* (Putnam's, 1934), 109; C.S. Lewis, *An Experiment in Criticism* (Cambridge University Press, 1961), 131–132; Thomas G. Long, *Preaching and the Literary Forms of the Bible* (Fortress, 1989), 13–15.

4 Although some distinguish the two, I use "genre" and "form" interchangeably in this book.

of literature differently. Genre-sensitivity is an essential part of reading competence.

Unfortunately, we do not always preach Scripture the way we read Scripture. The genre-sensitivity with which we approach the varied forms of biblical literature is shelved when we craft sermons on those forms. We make the sophomoric mistake of thinking that when you paraphrase a poem you have said the same thing in different words. What we read in the study is, "The Lord is my Shepherd." What we say in the pulpit is, "God can be counted on to provide for his people." And we do not realize that the sermon has *not* said what the text says. The affective, imaginative, and aesthetic appeal of the original line is forgotten, down the hall in our study.

What has probably happened is that we have learned to preach just one genre of sermon. We have grown comfortable with a preaching form that works well with, say, epistolary material, and then tried to make that form work for every genre of Scripture. Sermons on proverbs sound like sermons on Philippians; sermons on psalms sound like sermons on Luke. Every week it's three main points, or problem/solution, or perhaps even a narrative structure—a welcome alternative to the older propositional preaching, but one which can all too easily become a new rut. Sunday after Sunday we cram parables and proverbs, laments and lyrics into our homiletical grinders and out comes something that tastes just like last week's sausage.

Preachers will never do justice to the psalms until we put to rest the notion that a single sermon form will fit the varied forms of biblical literature. We already know that form and content cannot be separated in literature; why should it be any different when it comes to speaking that literature anew in the pulpit? When we mine a biblical poem for "ideas" or "principles" and then preach *those* in a form not representative of the text, we cheat listeners out of much of the Spirit-intended impact of the psalm.

A More Excellent Way

The alternative is to preach biblically: "Let doxologies be shared doxologically, narratives narratively, polemics polemically, poems poetically, and parables parabolically. In other words, biblical preaching ought to be biblical."[5] Fred Cradock's oft-quoted appeal to let the shape of the text shape the sermon is seconded by Gene Tucker:

> It has been taken more or less for granted that the *content* of the sermon should in some way conform to that of the text. Equally important is the relationship between the *form* of the text and that of the sermon. What mood, shape, genre, style, and tone is consistent with the text? Can the sermon, by being shaped by the literary features of the text, evoke the same response as the text does?[6]

> Let biblical preaching be biblical—in form as well as content. Let sermons on psalms be psalmish—in form as well as content.[7]

This is not to say that every sermon must assume the same shape as its text, so that a sermon on a psalm must itself be a poem, a sermon on a prayer be a prayer, a sermon on a hymn be sung, and so forth. Clearly, this would often prove impractical. What matters is that the Spirit-intended effect of the text—a product of form and content which is greater than either alone—be experienced in the hearing of the sermon. The idea is not to replicate the form of the text, but to respect it, to treat its literary features not as discardable chaff, but as significant factors in the choices we'll make in shaping the sermon.[8] "How," preachers will want to ask, "may the

---

5 Fred Craddock, *As One Without Authority*, 3rd ed. (Abingdon, 1981), 163.

6 Gene Tucker, "Reading and Preaching the Old Testament," in *Listening to the Word,* ed. Gail R. O'Day and Thomas G. Long (Abingdon, 1993), 138–139. See, too, Jeffrey Arthurs, *Preaching with Variety* (Kregel, 2007), 13–14.

7 This is not a new idea. Brian Daley notes that early Christian interpreters knew that psalms must receive special homiletical treatment if their unique poetic character would be preserved in sermons: "Finding the Right Key: The Aims and Strategies of Early Christian Interpretation of the Psalms," in *Psalms in Community*, ed. Harold W. Attridge and Margot Fassler (Society of Biblical Literature, 2003), 189–205.

8 Several authors who advocate genre-sensitive preaching clarify that they are not arguing for a kind of "formal fundamentalism," in which the sermon

sermon, in a new setting, say and do what the text says and does in its setting?"[9]

Well, what is it that psalm texts say and do? They engage listeners' emotions, imaginations, and aesthetic sense.

The Affective, Imaginative, and Aesthetic Concerns of the Psalms

Poetry knows that man does not live by propositions alone. It tries, more self-consciously than prose, to change us by moving our emotions, gripping our imaginations, and addressing our sense of beauty. These non-cognitive dimensions of texts are very much on the front burner in poetry.

Preachers, therefore, will want to figure out how sermons on poetic texts can engage affective, imaginative, and aesthetic sense, and will ask whether the literary features of the poems themselves may hold clues as to how such sermons might shape themselves.

Affect

The poem has been defined as the shortest emotional distance between two points—the writer and the reader. Poetry helps us notice, name, own, and affirm emotions. Or *heal* emotions: there are physicians who practice "poetry therapy" and note that the psalms in particular have served as potent medicine.[10] A rabbi and a social worker testify to the psychotherapeutic power of psalms, and note that it is the "poemness" of the psalms that makes the difference: "The Psalm is a song, 'a Song of the Soul.' As a song of the soul, it

---

replicates the form of the text: Fred B. Craddock, *Preaching* (Abingdon, 1985), 178; Thomas G. Long, *Preaching and the Literary Forms of the Bible* (Fortress, 1989), 34. Mike Graves (*The Sermon as Symphony* [Judson, 1997], 10, 18) proposes a helpful synonym for form-sensitive preaching: "re-presentational." Sermons that respect the form of the text do not settle for saying what the text says; they try to do what the text does, re-presenting the text in the preaching moment.

9 Long, *Preaching and the Literary Forms of the Bible,* 24 and 33.

10 Jack J. Leedy, ed., *Poetry Therapy* (Lippincott, 1969). See, too, Dennis Sylva, *Psalms and the Transformation of Stress,* Louvain Theological and Pastoral Monographs 16 (Eerdmans, 1995).

became necessary to render the emotional impact of the message through a creative vehicle—poetry rather than prose."[11]

But it is not just hurting and broken people who are touched by poetry. For all readers, the chief identifying trait of lyric poetry is its affective element. And psalms are lyrics. Sometimes they address our emotions directly by naming them: fear (Pss 2:11–12 and 5:7), joy (5:11; 21:6; 100:2), awe (Pss 8, 139), peace (4:8), comfort (119:76), contrition (51:17; 119:71), relief from distress (4:1; 20:1), confidence (27:3; 46:2–3), and hope (42:5) are among the emotions modeled, commended, or commanded in the Psalter. So is love for God's Word: "O how I love your law!" (119:97); "I delight in your decrees" (119:16). In these poetic lines, love may be more than emotion, but it is certainly not less. The psalmists found joy in Torah: "The precepts of the Lord are right, giving joy to the heart" (19:8). Following the example of the Hebrew poets, preaching on their compositions should cultivate joy in and love for the Word of God.

The psalmists acknowledge and express depression (32:3–4), broken heartedness (34:18), soul weariness (119:28), anger (109:1–3, 6–12), anxiety (12:1; 22:1), keen longing (143:7) and deep sorrow (Pss 6 and 88). They curse and praise, celebrate and adore, they cry, they complain, they exult, they bless, and they invite us to join them. John Calvin spoke for many who have let the Hebrew poets touch them deeply: "I have been accustomed to call this book, I think not inappropriately, 'An Anatomy of all Parts of the Soul;' for there is not an emotion of which any one can be conscious that is not here represented as in a mirror."[12]

Psalms not only speak to our emotions directly by naming them. More often they make their affective appeal indirectly. They do not say "Feel awe," but paint an awe-inspiring picture (Psalm 18). They do not say, "Feel at peace," but give us the pastoral imagery of Psalm 23. The repeated "How long?" of Psalm 13, the cadenced praise of Torah in Psalm 19, the aural imagery of Psalm

11 Joseph H. Gelbermann and Dorothy Kobak, "The Psalms as Psychological and Allegorical Poems," in *Poetry Therapy*, ed. Leedy, 133.

12 John Calvin, *Commentary on the Book of Psalms*, trans. James Anderson (Eerdmans, 1998), 1:xxxvi–xxxvii.

98—in short, the poetics of psalms—carry emotive weight greater than any prosaic rendition of these same truths.

Readers and preachers who are more at home with straightforward prose may be surprised to learn that poets sometimes choose language truer to the *emotion* they want to convey than to the literal scene being depicted.[13] The psalmists know, for instance, that the Maker of heaven and earth does not sleep (Psalm 121), yet they cry "Awake, O Lord!" (Pss 7:6; 35:23; 44:23; cf. 78:65). They know that Yahweh is a covenant-keeping God (89:34), yet at times they feel as though he has reneged on his covenant (44:9, 17–18). This is not confused theology but authentically emotive speech.

To quibble over the psalmists' hyperbole when depicting sorrow and trouble because they are not speaking the literal truth would be just plain silly: of course David's couch was not literally drenched with tears (3:6), of course he didn't literally eat ashes (102:9). We know that he was not literally drowning when overwhelmed by sadness (42:7) or when God rescued him from "deep waters" (18:16). The point of imagery and metaphor is emotive more than cognitive. "I am a worm and not a man" (22:6), "He makes Lebanon skip like a calf" (29:6), "The waters saw you and writhed" (77:16)—these expressions do not convey information like you might read in the *Gazette*; they convey emotion. There's danger, of course, in pressing this point too far, as if truth does not matter to the psalmists. These biblical poets were relentlessly theological. But that does not change the fact that poets, including biblical poets, often communicate feelings more directly than doctrinal claims.

Sometimes preachers should communicate feelings more directly than doctrinal claims. I once preached a sermon entitled "Awesome," based on Psalm 139. I wanted the congregation to know that God is awesome, but more importantly, I wanted them to *feel* God's awesomeness. The knowing and the feeling are inseparable: we're not interested in feelings divorced from the truth about which we're supposed to feel something, especially in a time when ignorance of sound theology is epidemic. As Jonathan

---

13 See John Ciardi, *How Does a Poem Mean?*, 2nd ed. (Houghton Mifflin, 1975), 205.

Edwards put it, when defending the emotional dimension of preaching during the Great Awakening, "I should think myself in the way of my duty, to raise the affections of my hearers as high as I possibly can, provided they are affected with nothing but the truth, and, with affections that are not disagreeable to the nature of what they are affected with."[14]

But it seemed to me that the poet's aim in writing Psalm 139, and therefore my aim in preaching Psalm 139, is primarily affective. His language embodies awe. It is breathless, amazed. Translators may or may not put exclamation points in our English versions, but we hear them in virtually every line of the poem: O Lord, you know! Such knowledge is too wonderful for me! Wherever I fly, you are there! Your works are wonderful! How vast, how precious! In four stanzas the poet masterfully portrays God the all-knowing, God the all-present, God the all-creative, and God the all-holy—God is awesome!

In preaching this text I tried to be as awe-struck as the poet in language and tone. Delivery was fast-paced. Illustrations were brief, in keeping with the sense you get in this poem that "We cannot linger here; there's so much more to tell!" I shook my head in amazement at the words I spoke. Can you believe this? This is what God is like! My aim was that of another minister, who said of a message he preached, "The entire sermon has been an effort not just to tell people the truth but to help them feel it brushing up against the walls of their hearts."[15]

A fuller discussion of *how* sermons can honor the emotional concerns of psalms can wait until chapter 7. For now it is enough to reiterate that if a psalm makes affective appeal a priority, so should a sermon on that psalm.

One of the chief ways poets convey emotion is by presenting situations or pictures which correlate with that emotion. So, not surprisingly, another mark of poetry is its imaginative appeal.

---

14 "Some Thoughts Concerning the Revival," in *The Great Awakening*, ed. C.C. Goen (Yale University Press, 1972), 387.

15 I believe the minister was Thomas Troeger, though I cannot find the original source.

Imagination

"Poems change what we think and feel not by piling up facts we did not know or persuading us through arguments, but by making finely tuned adjustments at deep and critical places in our imaginations."[16] Certainly this is true of biblical poems. Consider Psalm 42, for example, where "finely tuned adjustments" to our experience of God come through imagination. The poet does not pile up facts or argue a case for our need of God. He writes about a thirsty deer and a thirsty soul. He reminisces about leading worship and helps us picture the festive throng so we sympathize with his current isolation. We hear his groans and taste his tears. We feel the sights and sounds and spray of waterfalls and the echo of their tumult in his heart and our own, and sense something deeply symbolic about divine-human interaction. A pulpit exposition of this text that discarded its imaginative appeal and moved directly into prosaic theologizing would betray the poem and the Spirit who inspired it as *poetry*.

Prose, too, uses imagery, but in poetry the imagery is intensified and heightened, so that it becomes a distinguishing characteristic of poetic speech. Imaginative appeal is evident in dozens of psalms: God is seen as shepherd (23:1), shield (7:10), stronghold (9:9), rock (18:2), light (27:1), fortress (31:2–3), warrior (35:1–3), dwelling place (90:1), and shade (121:5), to cite just a few of the more common pictures. Imagery for God's actions include smashing the teeth of the wicked (3:7), raining fiery coals (11:6), thundering and shooting arrows (18:13–14), pitching a tent for the sun (19:4), anointing the poet's head (23:5), and breaking the cedars with the sound of his voice (29:5).

Readers of the psalms are invited to imagine human experience as falling into a pit (9:13), being calmed like a weaned child (131), and having their hearts turned to wax (22:14). Interpersonal harmony is imaged as oil running down Aaron's beard (133). Prayer is pictured as rising incense (141:2). People are broken pottery (31:12), withering grass (37:2), wineskins in smoke (119:83), or pillars carved to adorn a palace (144:2). Imaginative situations

---

16 Long, *Preaching and the Literary Forms of the Bible*, 45.

include narrow escape (124), gates opening to receive a king (24), God convening his heavenly court (82), and recording the nations in his book of the redeemed (87).

What is the preacher to do with all this imagery? Milk it for all its worth! Use it. Preach it. This abundance of poetic imagery is not ornamentation. It is not as though a skillful interpreter could render psalms prosaically without loss. God spoke and continues to speak through these images and intends that his spokesmen nourish his people's imaginations by speaking in the sermon through these same images.

Thomas Troeger lets the imaginative appeal of his text come through in a sermon on a line from Psalm 131 ("I have stilled and quieted my soul like a weaned child"). The sermon is entitled, simply, "Trust." Here's how Troeger begins.

Four lanes of traffic at sixty miles an hour. Tractor-trailers, family wagons, VW bugs, sports cars, pickup trucks, and our Greyhound bus were all driving as though the highway behind them were being rolled up like a carpet to be taken to the cleaners. If we didn't get out of the way fast enough, we would be rolled up with it.

Across the aisle in the bus a baby was sleeping. The mother had spread a diaper over her left shoulder and held the child there as if he were no burden at all.

The diesel's hum. Squealing brakes. Honking horns. The roar of rubber buffing concrete. Suicidal drivers who crossed without signaling from the far left-hand lane to exits on the right. None of these disturbed the child. He slept through it all.

Prayer is trusting God the way that child trusted his mother:

But I have calmed and quieted my soul,
like a child quieted at its mother's breast;
like a child that is quieted is my soul.[17]

---

17 Thomas Troeger, *Rage! Reflect. Rejoice!* (Westminster, 1977), 75. Troeger's sermon can be found in Appendix 2 of this book.

There are plenty of preachers who might introduce a sermon this way (though we're not all as good with words as Troeger is). But many would then leave behind the imagery of the illustration and the psalm and get on with the real business of preaching: "explaining" the word picture in ordinary prose. Sure, sermon introductions require something snappy to get people's attention, but then we can do what we came here to do: reason, argue, defend, prove, and apply.

Troeger, however, lets the image of the trustful child shape his entire sermon. This picture is not decoration, but root, trunk, and branch of the sermon. Troeger returns again and again to the baby on the bus and the child in the psalm, to the mother and the God who is like that mother. He uses language drawn from the image, speaking of our temptation to a driven lifestyle ("we keep driving on"), our reluctance to slow down and pray ("our revved up motors"), how hard it is not to concern ourselves with "matters too great for us" ("if we took our eyes off the road for one second, we could get clobbered by the fool who is tailgating us or the van that wants to squeeze between us and the orange Camaro").

"Trust" in this sermon is not an abstraction coolly examined in the lecture hall but a choice to leave the driving to someone who knows what he's doing. Prayer is not a philosophical topic but a decision to relax while the rest of the world moves at breakneck speed. The issue raised for all who listen to this psalm and sermon is whether or not we will live like that child in traffic, unperturbed, resting in the wisdom and competence of his mother. By sermon's end we have been carried by the poem and the preacher's imaginative treatment of it out of the typical sermonic world of pure idea and into the world of sense experience.

Alonso Schökel said "What has been written with imagination must also be read with imagination, provided the individual has imagination and it is in working order."[18] What has been written and then read with imagination must be preached with imagination, provided the preacher has imagination and it is in working order!

---

18 Luis Alonso Schökel and Adrian Graffy, *A Manual of Hebrew Poetics* (Gregorian Biblical Press, 1988), 104.

Aesthetics

Though he was no friend of biblical religion, H. L. Mencken said that "the Bible is unquestionably the most beautiful book in the world."[19] This should not surprise us, since the Bible comes to us from One who *is* Beauty, who made the world beautiful and his image-bearers capable of experiencing beauty. The artistry of the Bible reflects the nature of its divine Author and the nature of its incomparable message.

The psalms, in particular, have earned high praise. Their self-consciousness about form and rhythm and image and metaphor demonstrates that their composers did not intend to write bland, efficient memoranda. As seventeenth-century author George Wither put it,

> As the Psalms are excellent in regard of the Author and Matter of them; so are they also in respect of their Forme. And, in my opinion, it addeth somewhat to their dignitie, that they doe by a sweete and extraordinary kind of speaking, seeke to ravish the minde with the love of God; and through the delicate Harmony of words, so allure men unto his praises, that, notwithstanding the tediousness which flesh and blood findeth in that exercise, they are by degrees wont to doe it with some good measure of chearefulness.[20]

This accolade, almost as old as the King James Version, reminds us that not only do we have in the Psalter a priceless literary treasure, but that for *pastoral* reasons we cannot afford to ignore the aesthetics of biblical poetry. Beauty "allures" people to the praise of God, even when praising God is unnatural for us in our present state. Virtue can be "tedious," but when commended in a way that strikes us as beautiful, it just might be practiced with a "measure of

---

19 Alex Preminger and Edward L. Greenstein, eds., *The Hebrew Bible in Literary Criticism* (Ungar, 1986), 286.

20 George Wither, quoted in Preminger and Greenstein, eds., *The Hebrew Bible in Literary Criticism,* 527.

chearefulness." Basil of Caesarea recognized this crucial aesthetic value of the psalms in the fourth century:

> When the Holy Spirit saw that the human race was guided only with difficulty toward virtue, and that, because of our inclination toward pleasure, we were neglectful of an upright life, what did he do? The delight of melody he mingled with the doctrines, so that by the pleasantness and softness of the sound we might receive without perceiving it the benefit of the words, just as wise physicians, who, when giving the fastidious rather bitter drugs to drink, frequently smear the cup with honey.[21]

Beauty contributes to and enhances the intended effect of poetic texts (and sermons on those texts), because life is experienced not only as right and wrong, true and false, but as beautiful and ugly. We are attracted to or repulsed by truth claims or world-views or ethical requirements according to their *aesthetic* quality. It may matter little to a bored congregation how cogently the preacher argues the truth claims of a biblical text if there's nothing attractive about that truth or its presentation. The beauty of God and his Word is a homiletical issue because preachers must not only convince people of the truth but commend the truth as winsome, appealing, and existentially viable. We want listeners to say not only, "I see that you're right," but "What a beautiful way to live!"

The psalmists knew this. They did not negate their message by writing ugly poems about beautiful realities. They crafted every line, choosing words with utmost care. That took effort, but oh, what delightful effort!

Robert Frost once gave a public reading of his work and then agreed to field questions. Someone asked about the mechanics of writing, and Frost answered with evident relish, happy to have at least one listener who shared his enthusiasm for scansion, simile, synecdoche, and so on. A woman in the audience, however, was

---

21 Brian Daley cites Basil's "Homily on Psalm 1" as one who knew that the Psalms must be handled differently if their unique poetic character is to be preserved in sermons: "Finding the Right Key" in *Psalms in Community*, ed. Attridge and Fassler, 196.

obviously not tracking with him. Disillusioned and agitated, she interrupted, "Surely, Mr. Frost, you do not mean to say that when you are writing one of your beautiful poems (and she drew out the word 'bee-oot-i-ful') you're actually thinking about all these *technical tricks*." Frost leaned forward, and in his trademark gravelly voice said, "Madam, I revel in 'em!"[22]

It was, of course, his "reveling" that made Frost's poems bee-oot-i-ful. And presumably the Hebrew poets reveled in the technical tricks of their craft.[23] We may well imagine that it gave them pleasure to figure out how to say what they wanted to say—creatively and within the limits imposed by the structures of poetic convention. What a shame it would be to waste their efforts by a prosaic treatment of their art in our preaching.

A "homiletic of distillation"[24] treats the literary artistry of the Bible as nice but nonessential to its meaning and therefore nonessential to its preaching. Such an approach is wrong on both counts. We cannot understand, let alone preach artistic texts—and the psalms are manifestly artistic texts—if we miss their aesthetic dimension.

> Truth and beauty are in the Scriptures, as indeed they must always be, an inseparable unity. . . . Scripture is maligned and misinterpreted when its aesthetic quality is ignored in favor of exclusively expository and didactic interpretation. Is it not equally wrong to handle the Scripture unaesthetically as to handle it untruthfully?[25]

We who preach the psalms should be as conscientious in handling their artistic form as we are with their theology. We will craft and

---

22 The story is related by John Ciardi, *How Does a Poem Mean?* xix–xx.

23 "On the whole, I think we have given insufficient credit to the poet for the subtleties and intricacies in his artistic creation, and it is better to err on that side for a while. If we find some clever device or elaborate internal structure, why not assume that the poet's ingenuity, rather than our own, is responsible?" David Freedman, "Another Look at Biblical Poetry," in *Directions in Hebrew Poetry,* ed. Elaine R. Follis (JSOT Press, 1987), 8.

24 The phrase is Richard Eslinger's. *A New Hearing* (Abingdon, 1987), 66.

25 Clyde Kilby, *Christianity and Aesthetics* (IVP, 1961), 20–21.

wordsmith our sermons not to draw attention to ourselves, not to display homiletical virtuosity, but to invite our listeners to behold the fair beauty of the Lord.

The aesthetic concerns of the psalms can be seen not only in their exquisite artistry, but in the claims they make about the Word of God and our experience of God. They describe Scripture as "precious" (19:10), "sweet" (119:103), and "flawless silver" (12:6). In keeping it there is "great reward" (19:11). Torah is better than gold and is the theme of the psalmist's song (119:14, 54, 72, 127). C.S. Lewis, commenting on this psalm, says this "is the language of a man ravished by moral beauty."[26]

If God's Word is beautiful, so is God's presence (26:8; 84:1) and strength (21:1). His providence, the psalmists testify, is "pleasant" and "delightful" (16:6). They long to be filled with the good things of God's house (65:4), to enjoy fellowship with him (16:11), and "to gaze upon the beauty of the Lord" (27:4).

One way to raise listeners' consciousness of beauty is to do as the psalmists do: use the vocabulary of beauty. James Howell preached a sermon on Psalm 27:4 ("to gaze upon the beauty of the Lord") in which he said the words "beauty" or "beautiful" over fifty times. He spoke of the beauty of God, the beauty of holiness, the beauty of Scripture, the beauty of God's sanctuary or any place where his people gather for worship. Of course, using the vocabulary of beauty would not have been enough by itself. Howell's sermon was also beautifully designed and executed; it included imaginative depictions of beauty and evoked a longing like that of the psalmist for an experience of God that is, in the most profound sense of the word, aesthetic.[27]

The Hebrew poets invite readers to "delight" in God's truth (1:2; 119:24) and in the congregation of his people (16:3); to "taste and see that the Lord is good" (34:8); to rejoice in his honor" (149:5) and to worship him "in the splendor of his holiness" (29:2; 96:9). Every exhortation to praise the Lord is an invitation to aesthetic response: we are called upon to admire the One who is supremely

---

26 *Reflections on the Psalms* (Harcourt, 1958), 60.

27 The sermon is in Dave Bland and David Fleer, eds., *Performing the Psalms* (Chalice, 2005), 131–140.

admirable. "It is *good* (Hebrew *tob*)," Psalm 92 says, "to praise the Lord and to make music to your name, O Most High." The Hebrew word *tob* can mean "beautiful" as well as "good," so Weiser comments, ". . . this shows to what a high degree the aesthetic and the ethical and religious aspects of the worshipping life are here comprehended as a unity by those who are subject to the vivid impression produced by the glory of God."[28] What God has joined together, let not the preacher put asunder.

To artistic purists who might object that art is for art's sake and should not be pressed into the service of religious persuasion, Henry Mitchell answers that all great art preaches: "This venerable western shibboleth [that art must be for art's sake] is found in no other culture of which I know, and is not even truly practiced among the elitists who espouse it. *All* powerful literature has a driving motivation behind it; the author is always involved in projecting a message."[29]

That projected message may be quite disturbing. Art may be beautiful, but that does not mean it is comforting or complacent. Totalitarian regimes are threatened by art, and so is the religious status quo.[30] Nothing said above about the attractiveness of biblical poetry implies that psalms are soothing or saccharine or safe. On the contrary, biblical poems are often ". . . *an assault on public imagination* aimed at showing that the present presumed world is not absolute, but that a thinkable alternative can be imagined, characterized and lived in."[31] It is doubtful whether preachers can communicate the disorienting, world-shaping vision of the biblical

---

28 Artur Weiser, *The Psalms,* trans. Herbert Hartwell (Westminster, 1962), 615.

29 *Celebration and Experience in Preaching* (Abingdon, 1990), 41. Wilder agrees: *Modern Poetry and the Christian Tradition* (Charles Scribner's Sons, 1952), 17.

30 Paul Scott Wilson, *Imagination of the Heart,* (Abingdon, 1998), 198.

31 Brueggemann, describing the prophetic task in "The Prophet as a Destabilizing Presence," in *The Pastor as Prophet,* ed. Earl E. Shelp and Ronald H. Sunderland (The Pilgrim Press, 1985), 51–52. Emphasis is in the original. That poetry is essential to the prophet's work is clear from Brueggemann's comments following this quote (p. 53) and in *The Prophetic Imagination* (Fortress, 1978).

poets without working hard at aesthetics in preaching.[32] Ministers who artfully craft their sermons on poetic texts are not prettying up their preaching; they are honoring these texts and enabling the kind of aesthetic/ethical/doxological response those texts were intended to evoke.

Emotion, imagination, and beauty—this is what the psalms are about, and what genre-sensitive preachers of the psalms should be about. The rest of this book offers fourteen homiletical strategies to help preachers honor the affective, imaginative, and aesthetic concerns of the psalms.

For Further Study

Arthurs, Jeffrey. *Preaching with Variety*. Kregel, 2007.
Wiersbe, Warren. *Preaching and Teaching with Imagination*. Victor, 1994.
Wardlaw, Don M., ed. *Preaching Biblically*. Westminster, 1983.
Long, Thomas G. *Preaching and the Literary Forms of the Bible*. Fortress, 1989.
Ryken, Leland. *Words of Delight*. Baker, 1992.
Ryken, Leland. "The Bible as Literature and Expository Preaching." Pages 38–53 in *Preach the Word*. Edited by Leland Ryken and Todd Wilson. Crossway, 2007.

Talk about It

Read the whole sermon Thomas Troeger preached on Psalm 131 (found in Appendix 2). How does his use of language engage your imagination?

Dig Deeper

Read or listen to other sermons on Psalm 131; compare and contrast their imaginative appeal with Troeger's.

---

32 Amos Wilder, *Theopoetic: Theology and the Religious Imagination* (Fortress, 1976), 1–3, 42.

Practice

Before reading the next chapter, look at Psalm 1. Jot down some
ideas for how a preacher might shape a sermon on this text so as to
preserve its poetic feel.

2

Image

Poetry is not the language of objective explanation but the language of imagination. It makes an image of reality in such a way as to invite our participation in it. We do not have more information after we read a poem, we have more experience. It is not "an examination of what happens but an immersion in what happens."[1]
Eugene Peterson

Strategy 1
Grow the Sermon from the Psalm's Imagery

When Thomas Troeger preached that sermon on Psalm 131, he didn't use the image of a sleeping child to "make a point" or to "illustrate" the sermon. The image *was* the sermon. Troeger knew that the text's image, "a weaned child with its mother," is the heart and soul of the psalm and needs to be the heart and soul of the sermon.

Not every psalm is so completely dominated by or dependent upon a single image. Some psalms have little imagery. Others employ multiple images, but in a supporting role. In several psalms,

---

1 Eugene Peterson, *Reversed Thunder: The Revelation of John and the Praying Imagination* (HarperCollins, 1988), 5. His quotation is from Denise Levertov, *The Poet in the World* (New Directions Publishing Corp., 1973), 239.

however, imagery plays such a vital role that a preacher should consider growing an entire sermon from it.

Take Psalm 1, for example. Two contrasting images introduce the two types of people we'll meet frequently in the hundred and forty-nine psalms that follow. Though something in us resists the notion that there are only two types of people in the world (we even tell jokes that begin with that line), Psalm 1 insists that this is the case. Though there's a time for saying with Solzhenitsyn that "the line dividing good and evil cuts through the heart of every man," Psalm 1 insists that a line separates two classes of people. What keeps this claim from being overly simplistic is the poem's imagery: the two types of people in the world are not just "good guys and bad guys," or even "the righteous" and "the wicked," though they are certainly that. They are tree people and chaff people. People with roots sunk deep into Torah—stable, solid, fruitful, and green—and people who are blown away with the least puff of wind because there's not much to them.

Tree people and chaff people. Now that's a sermon. I do not mean that I will mention these word pictures in passing, to lend a little color to a predominantly cognitive sermon. I mean that from beginning to end what listeners will encounter in the sermon are trees and chaff. What will hold the sermon together is not idea but image, not proposition but picture. When people go home from church, they will not be thinking, "It's good to be good and it's bad to be bad, so let's all try to be good," or even, "I must try to be more tree-like." The sermon will not have to say "we should" or "we must"; it will simply portray, as the poem does, two kinds of people and allow the picture itself to attract listeners to a tree kind of life, so that when they leave they will be praying "God make me a tree."

Preaching Psalm 1, I will try to paint a vivid picture of a tree person: Lucille Birk, perhaps, who discovers she has a tumor in her brain and only a few weeks to live, but who has been sinking her roots deep into the soil of God's Word for so many years that she's able to face this bleak prognosis unshaken. She has something to draw on now that she needs it. She bears fruit in this season of life—a testimony to all who know her that God is good and that life is more than health. She's a tree.

Then, too, I will sketch the chaff person (examples abound, though I probably will not name names). "Sketch" is the operative word here: I will not dwell too long on the chaff because the psalm does not dwell too long on the chaff. It is the tree that dominates this poem: three whole verses compared to one measly line about the chaff. Even the negatives of verse one, which could have been used in the portrait of the chaff, are used instead to describe what the tree person is not. The Hebrew describing the tree person is ponderous, hard to read rapidly; it slows the reader down so as to contemplate this impressive, deeply-rooted creature. "Not so the wicked." The words are spoken quickly and then, well, that's it; there's not a whole lot to say about the wicked. Just chaff. Celebrities come to mind, famous for being famous, but with no substance. In my sermon, chaff will get relatively little time, dismissed as of little importance ("the wicked will not stand") compared to the tree.

A sermon on Psalm 1 will certainly include ideas, propositions, truth claims, and reasons. But where a traditional sermon form would be shaped by these discursive elements and *contain* imagery, a genre-sensitive sermon is shaped by the imagery and contains the discursive elements.[2] The whole process of sermon development is governed not by rhetorical principles: "What's the main idea? How can I develop it? What will be the main points of the sermon, and, oh, by the way, how does the imagery fit in?"—but by poetics: "How can I work with this poem to portray tree people and chaff people?"[3]

Several other psalms feature imagery from which entire sermons can be grown: the shepherd of Psalm 23, the storm in Psalm 29, the heavenly court in Psalm 82, pilgrimage in Psalm 84, the eyes of a maid turned toward her mistress in Psalm 123, oil on

2 Eugene Lowry describes the "figure/ground shift" in homiletics. The older sermon form was a rhetorically shaped envelope containing poetics; the newer form is poetically shaped even though it contains rhetorical ingredients. This image of envelope and contents summarizes as neatly as anything I've read the revolution in homiletics. "The Revolution of Sermonic Shape," in *Listening to the Word,* ed. Gail O'Day and Thomas G. Long (Abingdon, 1993), 111–112.

3 Preachers will want to begin playing with images even while the sermon is in its embryonic stages. Imagination cannot be hurried, but requires brooding time. Paul Scott Wilson, *Imagination of the Heart* (Abingdon, 1998), 49–50.

Aaron's beard and dew on Hermon in Psalm 133. An image-shaped
sermon might be grown from any of these. Or from the "rock" in
Psalm 18. "Rock" will not be a picture on display for a moment or
two before the preacher hurries to distill from "rockness" concepts
like stability or firmness. "Rock" makes the sermon. "Rock" is repeated, drummed into the listener's consciousness. "Rock" is what
we feel under foot, or—if we conclude that in this case the rock is a
high crag to which the poet can flee—we imagine ourselves hidden
in this unassailable refuge. "Rock" is the vision of the poet and the
preacher; it becomes the vision of the people.

Psalm 87 paints what may be the most striking image in the entire Psalter: God recording in his Registry of the Redeemed names
from Israel's pagan neighbors and enemies! The poem begins with
an affirmation every Israelite would accept as a given: God loves
Zion. Glorious things are spoken of her. But then—what a shocking twist!—we hear the "glorious things" spoken of Zion: "This
one and that one were born in her," people from Egypt, Babylon,
Philistia, Tyre, and Cush. What on earth are *these* people doing in
God's book?

I preached a sermon on this text entitled, "Birth Announce-
ments," using the church's membership roll (a literal book that's
been kept for decades) as a prop and inviting the congregation to
warmly recall some of the entries in it. Then I challenged them to
reflect on some of the names God might want to enter in that book
in our day—names we would never have thought to write there.
Our neighborhood was changing ethnically, and the psalm posed
the question of whether we share God's joy over the unexpected
names he's recording in his register of Zion. The imagery of the
poem was not a feature of the sermon; it *made* the sermon.

Imagery is not necessarily visual. Psalm 42, for example, facilitates not only imaginative sight (with its picture of the deer),
but imaginative touch (thirst and near drowning) and imaginative sound (deep calling to deep). Psalm 148 is rich in aural imagery, and so is Elizabeth Achtemeier's sermon on that text, "God
the Music Lover."[4] Through skillfully chosen images she helps

4 The sermon is found in Elizabeth Achtemeier, *Nature, God, and Pulpit*
(Eerdmans, 1992), 40–49.

listeners hear the music of creation and grieve the silencing of that music through ecological irresponsibility. Her sermon is not merely enriched by this imagery of sound—it depends on it.

Consider the possibilities for growing a sermon from the aural imagery of Psalm 59. Enemies, who feature in so many psalms, appear in this one as vicious dogs. The poet imagines not so much the deeds of the dogs but their sound: they spew threats and swords. They threaten the psalmist by "the sins of their mouths," "the words of their lips," "the curses and lies they utter." They slink out of their hiding places at night and keep the poet awake with their snarling and howling.

In a sermon entitled "Drowning Out the Dogs," one preacher makes creative use of this psalm's aural imagery. Several times he helps listeners hear the fearful night noises of the "dogs" in their personal lives and in a world still hostile toward God's people as it was in David's day. The sermon also develops the imagery of God's scornful laughter (v.8) and the psalmist's confident praise (vv.16-17), both of these sounds louder and more enduring than the threats of the dogs. These hopeful sounds may for us, as for the poet, "drown out the dogs." Imaginative appeal is not just an introductory motif or concluding tack-on; it gives the sermon coherence from start to finish.

A psalm might present a sequence of images without developing them at length. In this case the preacher will probably not grow an entire sermon from any one image, but will let the sermon move with and by means of the series. Psalm 46 serves as an example. The poem's movements defy rational step-by step exposition. This text moves, and moves us, by means of a sequence of images: refuge, earthquake, a "river whose streams make glad the city of God," a fortress, war, a voice from "outside" the psalm ("Be still and know that I am God") then a fortress again.

A sermon on this text should not flatten its poetry into prose, but will seek to recreate the poem's sequence of images and their effects. The preacher will help listeners respond emotionally and imaginatively to the earthquake, river, battle, and especially the fortress. As Troeger summarizes: "If God communicates with you through an image, then that tells you something about how to let

God speak through you to the congregation. Share the vision you received!"[5]

Strategy 2
Speak in Pictures

What if, in a given psalm, imagery is not so prominent as to be its defining characteristic? Should the preacher try to grow an entire sermon from an image if the poet himself does not make that much of it? Probably not. But that does not mean the imagery that is there can be ignored or paraphrased away. In many psalms, imagery is not so fully developed that it begs to be made into a whole sermon, but it should still be spoken anew in the sermon.

For example, I was struck recently by a brief word picture in Psalm 33:7, "He gathers the waters of the sea into jars." I've lived much of my life near the ocean, and I assure you that you cannot "gather it" into anything. Take every jar in your house down to the beach, borrow jars from all your neighbors, fill them up, and you will not diminish the sea one little bit. Three quarters of the earth's surface is covered with water. When even the surface of the deep moves, you get out of the way. Yet God collects the seas into jars for his storehouses.

Now, if I were preaching Psalm 33, I would probably not do an entire sermon sensationally entitled "JARS!" The image does not merit that much attention. But neither would I want to make too little of it, cheating my congregation out of the imaginative, emotive power of this brief word picture. I'll use it in my sermon in proportion to the way the psalmist does in his poem—no more but no less.

In Psalm 121:6 we find a nice example of merismus (a figure of speech which uses contrasting parts to stand for the whole, such as "from the crown of his head to the sole of his foot," which refers to the entire person): "The sun will not harm you by day, nor the moon by night." The psalmist could have written, and a preacher could say, "Nothing will ever hurt you." But even if we argue that this paraphrase means roughly the same *thing* as the metaphor, it

---

5 Thomas Troeger, *Creating Fresh Images for Preaching* (Judson, 1982), 18.

does not mean the same *way*. "Sun" and "moon" communicate differently than the more abstract "nothing." "By day" and "by night" work differently from the paraphrase "ever." The poetic figure makes the truth more vivid and memorable, and the sermon will try to do likewise, imaging the threats of daytime and nighttime and God's ability to deal with any and all of them.

Sometimes the imagery we encounter in the psalms is literal—part of the lived experience of the original audience—and the poet assumes what we cannot assume so many centuries later, that his imagery will be understood. Take, for example, images of water or drought. We who live in fertile, well-watered parts of the world may not appreciate the dryness of Negev, or how vital the autumn and winter rains were in the psalmists' world. When preaching a psalm that features drought, rain, or thirst, we may have to provide a more detailed picture where the poet gave only a sketch, so that the emotive, imaginative power of the poem will not be lost on our hearers.

Mountains form part of the landscape in several psalms. Do our listeners know that the psalmists' world, a rather narrow slice of real estate, was dominated by a 2,000-3,000 foot ridge running north to south? Can they appreciate what these references to mountains are meant to evoke? We may have to paint a mental picture where the psalmist uses only a word or two. Where the poet of Psalm 29 hears the voice of God in thunder and lightning moving in from the northwest, we might have to take some pulpit time to locate Lebanon and Kadesh and help listeners follow the progress of this awesome storm.

The images and metaphors of Israel's hymn book are richer and more varied than we might suppose if we only know the most familiar psalms. But compared with, say, an anthology of "150 Best Loved Poems," the Psalter's stock is limited to a small and uncomplicated assortment.[6] That fact might disappoint the literati, but the simplicity of the psalms' imagery is a boon to all who pray and

---

6 A useful tool for any Bible student is the *Dictionary of Biblical Imagery*, ed. Leland Ryken, James C. Wilhoit, and Tremper Longman III (InterVarsity, 1998). Hundreds of images and figures are explained and traced through the Scriptures.

preach them.[7] The most unliterary believer can understand that
God is a rock, refuge, shepherd, or king. The simplest reader can
imagine a pillow drenched with tears. Anyone can identify with
drowning in grief, or imagine what it would feel like to be sur-
rounded by lions or trapped in a cave. All of us know the pleasures
of the table.

Eugene Peterson writes that when praying the imagery of the
Psalms:

> We use ordinary language spoken and understood by any five
> year old. There is no chance of pretense in using these words,
> of pretending that our understanding of our relationship to
> God depends on special insights or secret codes. . . . By us-
> ing language in prayer that everyone else uses when they are
> not praying, we are kept in community with them. Nothing is
> more socializing than common speech; nothing more clique
> forming than jargon. The Psalms, by profuse and insistent use
> of metaphor, make it as difficult as they possibly can for us to
> sally off into vague abstractions, contemptuous of the actual
> grass under our feet, and call this verbal woolgathering prayer.[8]

We might add that psalms, by profuse and insistent use of metaphor
and imagery, make it as difficult as they possibly can for ministers
to sally off into vague generalities and call this prosaic speechifying
a sermon. "It is by imagination that men have lived; imagination
rules all our lives. The human mind is not, as philosophers would

---

7 Robert Alter observes that, "the biblical poets on the whole were inclined
to draw on a body of more or less familiar images without consciously striving for
originality of invention in their imagery" ("Ancient Hebrew Poetry," in *The Literary Guide to the Bible*, ed. Robert Alter and Frank Kermode (Harvard University
Press, 1987), 517. Alter believes that the conventional imagery of the Psalms is
suited to their intended use: obscure or daring departures from what the average
worshipper could readily grasp would defeat their devotional/liturgical purpose.
Conventional or not, the images of the Psalms speak powerfully and memorably
to the heart. And what they lack in the precision of literal speech they compen-
sate for in vividness.

8 Eugene Petersen, *Answering God: The Psalms as Tools for Prayer* (Harper-
Collins, 1989), 77.

have you think, a debating hall, but a picture gallery."[9] Preaching psalms with their wealth of imagery gives preachers an opportunity to change some of the pictures hanging in our listeners' minds. Some of them probably picture God as the effeminate Jesus of early twentieth century religious art; they need the divine warrior imagery of Psalms 18, 35 and others to correct this misleading mental image. Some of our people are "in the pits"; they need to see and feel and smell the pit David was in (Ps 9) and be freed to express as honestly as he did their grief and fear. Some in the congregation are anxious or guilt-ridden; the preacher may do them more good by unfolding the hopeful watchman imagery of Psalm 130 than by a prosaic exhortation to "stop fretting!"

There's risk involved in preaching metaphorically. If the image is foreign to us or if the metaphor can be interpreted in more than one way, some listeners may not understand. A preacher might be inclined to play it safe, like one writer Samuel Johnson complained about: "The rogue never hazards a metaphor."[10] Preachers might hesitate to "hazard a metaphor" because we cannot guarantee its intended meaning will be grasped. But what a prosaic style gains in safety and clarity it loses in imaginative punch. Some degree of risk is the price to be paid for a powerful communicative effect: with metaphor, hearers are required to become active partners in the discovery of meaning rather than passive recipients of meaning.[11]

Care should be taken, however, not to overdose on metaphors. Too many make for purple prose. And worse, "Listeners cannot handle the mental gymnastics involved in too many metaphorical

---

9 John R.W. Stott (quoting MacNeille Dixon), *Between Two Worlds* (Eerdmans, 1982), 282–283.

10 Richard E. Hughes and P. Albert Duhamel, "Rhetorical Qualities of Words," in *Selected Readings in Public Speaking,* ed. Jane Blankenship and Robert Wilhoit (Dickenson Publishing, 1966), 148.

11 "Metaphor and simile place immense demands on a reader. They require far more activity than a direct propositional statement does. They therefore involve far greater risk on the part of the writer, who entrusts a significant part of the act of communication to the reader." Leland Ryken, *Words of Delight* (Baker, 1992), 168. See too, Ryken, "Metaphor in the Psalms," *Christianity and Literature* 21, no. 3 (1982): 22–23, Schökel's comments on the risks involved in interpreting images, *A Manual of Hebrew Poetics* (Pontifical Biblical Institute, 1988), 100–101.

allusions.["12] Balance is needed: if the preacher plays it safe, the sermon will be prosaic and flat in comparison with the poetic text; but if listeners are in a fog because the sermon is a cavalcade of images, all pictures and no propositions, the preacher has not served the congregation or the gospel very well. A genre-sensitive sermon on a psalm, however poetic and creative its style, cannot be a series of disconnected metaphors and images.

Another word of caution: be careful about substituting a different metaphor for the one the psalmist chose. The first time I preached on Psalm 1, I decided that since chaff is foreign to my contemporaries I would substitute dandelions. I preached about "Tree People and Dandelion People." I was thinking of the dandelion puff that the wind blows away, but afterward a helpful listener told me that when he thinks of dandelions he thinks about their tenacious roots and how hard it is to eradicate them from his lawn – definitely not the associations the psalmist was evoking with his image of chaff! The next time I preached this text, I used the poet's image instead of a potentially misleading substitute.

If Warren Wiersbe was right, many pastors have only themselves to blame if congregations listen to their sermons week after week with little life change to show for it. Overly cognitive preaching has left God's people with starved imaginations.[13] Whatever we may do with other genres, at least when we preach the psalms we can nourish imaginations by growing entire sermons from the imagery of the text or, at least, speaking in pictures.

For Further Study

Brown, William P. *Seeing the Psalms: A Theology of Metaphor*. Westminster John Knox, 2002.

Ryken, Leland, James C. Wilhoit, Tremper Longman III, eds. *Dictionary of Biblical Imagery*. InterVarsity, 1998.

---

12 Lowry, *How to Preach a Parable*, 63. On too much of a good thing, see William Kooienga, *Elements of Style for Preaching* (Zondervan, 1989), 93; Paul Scott Wilson, *The Practice of Preaching* (Abingdon, 1995), 236.

13 Warren W. Wiersbe, *Preaching and Teaching with Imagination* (Victor, 1994), 60–61.

Troeger, Thomas. *Creating Fresh Images for Preaching.* Judson, 1982.

Troeger, Thomas. *Imagining a Sermon.* Abingdon, 1990.

Talk about It

Read a couple of entries from the *Dictionary of Biblical Imagery* on some common images in the psalms (rock, horn, fortress, for example). What do you learn from these articles that might easily be missed in prosaic sermons that do not make good use of the images?

Dig Deeper

Preachers should not limit their reading to theology. We need to read fiction and poetry to develop a feel for how words are used. Maybe this week would be a good time to add a collection of poems to the stack on your night table. You might start with Robert Frost who is very accessible.

Practice

Write a paragraph or two for a sermon on Psalm 121, using the imagery of verse 6 ("The sun will not harm you by day, nor the moon by night"). Remember that using the imagery of a poem in a sermon does not mean *talking about* the image—describing trees and chaff, for instance. It means *using* the image to paint a picture of the reality it images. In this writing exercise, you want to use day and night, sun and moon to vividly re-create the reality the poet means to image.

3

Moves

Most emphatically the Psalms must be read as poems; as lyrics, with all the licenses and all the formalities, the hyperboles, the emotional rather than logical connections which are proper to lyric poetry.[1]
C.S. Lewis

Strategy 3
Follow the Logic of the Poem

Follow the logic of the poem? Aren't "logic" and "poem" mutually exclusive? You might think so, the way the terms are ordinarily used: "The Psalms must be read as poems . . . with all the . . . emotional rather than logical connections."[2] "The Hebrew thinks with the eye; the connection is optical rather than logical."[3] "Systematic persons, forgetting that they are reading poetry, may be puzzled by the frequent lack of a logical sequence of ideas in any one Psalm ...."[4]

Is "logic of poetry" an oxymoron?

It depends on what we mean by logic. Certainly the logic of poetry is not the logic of philosophical discourse or debate. Psalms do not move from proposition to proof to implications. Line two

---

1 C.S. Lewis, *Reflections on the Psalms* (Harcourt Brace Jovanovich, 1958), 3.

2 Ibid.

3 John Patterson, *The Praises of Israel* (Charles Scribner's Sons, 1950), 24.

4 Donald Macleod, "Preaching from the Psalms," in *Biblical Preaching*, ed. James W. Cox (Westminster, 1983), 107.

does not follow line one syllogistically. You will not hear a psalmist say, "My third point, which follows logically from the second ...."[5]

Nor is the logic of poetry the logic of narrative. Psalms do not tell stories. Not usually, anyway (a few "historical" psalms are exceptions)—not the kind of stories we find in Genesis or Samuel. Their connections are not chronological; their development does not depend on plot. The poet's job is not to tell us what *happened*, but what *happens*.[6] Robert Alter makes a helpful distinction: "What the poets give us is not narrative but narrativity—which is to say, the narrative development of metaphor."[7] The psalmist does not set out to narrate an event but to paint a picture. It may be a *moving* picture, as in Psalm 18 where God parts the heavens and comes down to rescue the psalmist, riding the cherubim, soaring, thundering, shooting arrows. But it is still a picture, not a story.

In the late twentieth century, narrative became a deservedly popular mode of preaching. Preachers everywhere began telling stories. But in our enthusiasm for this approach—a theologically faithful and intrinsically interesting approach—we need to be careful that we do not replace traditional sermon structure with narrative as a new one-size-fits-all homiletic. The Bible includes a variety of genres, and preaching the Bible requires a variety of homiletical strategies suited to these genres.

Narrativity, not Narrative

Consider Psalm 118. Clearly, a story lies behind this poem, a story of deliverance from enemies (vv. 5–7, 10–12). But if the psalmist had wanted to tell this story, he would have given us more detail.

---

5 J. Clinton McCann and James C. Howell offer insightful suggestions on the way poems move and how sermons on poems, therefore, ought to move: *Preaching the Psalms* (Abingdon, 2001), chapter 5.

6 Northrop Frye, *The Educated Imagination* (Indiana University Press, 1964), 63.

7 Robert Alter, *The Art of Biblical Poetry* (Harper-Collins, 1985), 39. Paul Scott Wilson discusses the history-like character of some biblical genres, "fictive plot," as a paradigm for narratizing Psalms for preaching. "Reading the Psalms for Preaching," chapter 6 in *Performing the Psalms*, ed. Dave Bland and David Fleer (Chalice Press, 2005), 105–120.

He would have preserved tension and postponed until just the right moment in the narration, what Tolkien called the "euca-tastrophe" or turning point. But as it is he sketches only the barest detail and gives away the outcome right from the start. He begins with thanksgiving for a deliverance already experienced, a deliverance we didn't even know he needed.

Sometimes a narrator may choose to begin at the end of his story and "flash back." But the poet of Psalm 118 does not really do this. He moves from call to worship to a brief mention of unnamed enemies, then on to praise, affirmation of faith, and back again to a call to worship. The strict envelope structure—verbatim repetition of the poem's first line at the end—is not common in the psalms, but it fits here. The poet completes a circuitous route from thanks-giving to thanksgiving, recounting in-between how his personal experience justifies the refrain, "Give thanks to the Lord, for he is good; his love endures forever."

This is not the logic of narrative, but what we might call the logic of testimony, the kind of movement we see when a friend whose story we already know relates again those parts of her conversion experience that are relevant at the moment. Or when someone in a prayer meeting tells about his battle with cancer and urges us to join him in crediting God for healing. Details or chronology do not matter: we either know them already or they're not important for this occasion.

A preacher *could* plot a narrative sermon on Psalm 118, but why not follow the logic of the poem? Why not let the congrega-tion move with the psalmist from thanksgiving to testimony and back to thanksgiving, allowing the poem's movement and not just its ideas do its work in the sermon's hearers?

The Logic of Experience

A poem's development, if it is true to how we experience life, may not be rationally tidy. Psalm 74, for example, starts with a bold, almost bitter cry born out of national anguish (vv. 1–2). It moves on to complaint (vv. 3–10), climaxing with a plea found over and over in the psalms in varying words, "Lord, get your hands out of your pockets and do something!" Then, to the relief of every orthodox believer and every preacher who likes happy endings, the poet calms down and acknowledges confidence in God (vv. 12–17). Whew! We're sure glad/these biblical laments turn toward praise before they're done. We can bring this sermon in for a smooth landing, like countless others we have preached on the problem/solution model, and end the worship service in our culture's preferred mood of celebration.

But wait. The poem is not finished yet. It continues (regresses?) for six more verses, leaving behind the humble piety of the previous stanza and trying once more to tell God what to do. The poet is not content with recalling the good old days when God was in control, he issues a series of challenges, the gist of which is "God, are you going to take this sitting down?"

What are we to make of this in a sermon? Well, let's see, we have three stanzas here (vv. 1–11; 12–17; and 18–23). Good, we like three. We can work with three. Let's just rearrange things a bit, making the poet's third movement the sermon's second point. We'll deal with the two complaint sections of the poem first, then finish with the positive section, which the poet had placed in the middle. They did tell us in seminary that we do not always have to preach the text in the order it was written, that a psychologically satisfying arrangement of material may be preferable to verse-by-verse organization. This way we get three points *and* a happy ending.

No. Sometimes a sermon can legitimately juggle the order of the text. But not here, not now. It would not be honest preaching, and some listeners, at least, will sense it. This poem is true to life just the way it was written. This is how we pray sometimes, groping toward trust in God, voicing lament, then confidence, but with no guarantee that confidence will have the last word. The sermon should end where the text ends. This psalm's structure is the logic of authentic experience.

Outlining the Logic of Experience

A sermon on a psalm should rarely if ever be outlined the way we were taught in school to arrange didactic material:

I.

    A.

        1.

        2.

II.

    A. etc.

This sucks the life out of a poem. Outlines for sermons on psalms will block material according to the logic of the poem. Headings might name the images of the psalm instead of its "points." Indentations may represent a sequence of emotions in the poem. Sections may not look neatly parallel and proportional, because that is not how poetry presents life, all organized and tidy.

We might choose to outline not the text, but our *experience* as it was shaped by the text.[8] Let's say I'm preparing to preach Psalm 128 for Father's Day.

> Blessed are all who fear the LORD,
> > who walk in his ways.
> You will eat the fruit of your labor;
> > blessings and prosperity will be yours.
> Your wife will be like a fruitful vine
> > within your house;
> your sons will be like olive shoots
> > around your table.
> Thus is the man blessed
> > who fears the LORD.
> May the LORD bless you from Zion
> > all the days of your life;
> may you see the prosperity of Jerusalem,
> > and may you live to see your children's children.
> Peace be upon Israel.

Before consulting commentaries or putting pen to paper, I simply read the psalm aloud — several times—and listen. I listen to my

---

8 I am indebted to Thomas Troeger for this idea: "The Encounter of Text with Preacher," in *Preaching Biblically*, ed. Don Wardlaw (Westminster, 1983), 160.

own voice. I listen for the voice of the Spirit in the text. And I listen for the anticipated responses of my listeners. As I listen, I realize that some people in my congregation aren't too sure about my psalm. They aren't sure that they would call good what the psalmist calls good. Several grandparents who are forced to raise their grandkids wonder if living to "see your children's children" is really such a blessing. Not all the dads in the congregation wish they had more children "like olive shoots" around their table; they fret about feeding the one or two they already have. Not all of the mothers long to be more "like a fruitful vine"; many are doing their best to squelch their fertility. (A few, though, want desperately to conceive but cannot. Their voices, however, are almost lost in those of the crowd.) This is what I *hear* as I listen to the poem. What do I *see*? I see a pro-abortion bumper sticker on a car in our church parking lot. And another that reads, "AVENGE YOURSELF! LIVE LONG ENOUGH TO BE A BURDEN ON YOUR CHILDREN!" A kind of "thanks, but no, thanks" to the promise of the text.

It occurs to me that I inhabit a world different from that of the psalmist, an allegedly overpopulated world where small families seem to make sense, a world where not everyone considers children a blessing. I wonder if I will have to spend some sermon time talking about how this text does not apply to us in the same way it applied to a culture where large families were advantageous. I meditate for a while on this issue of cultural distance and its implications for my Father's Day sermon, but then I'm sidetracked by a question and by another mental picture.

The question: Are people today really all that different from the poet's first readers or do we exaggerate the differences because we've uncritically assimilated the values of our own time? Maybe the current disinclination to "replenish the earth" will prove to be a passing phase.

The picture: my father-in-law, a godly man, seated at Thanksgiving dinner with his wife, his six children and their spouses, and twenty-six grandchildren. Folding tables and chairs have been scrounged from the attic or borrowed from neighbors to stretch the dining room table out into the hall. Every serving dish they own is in use; few of us have matching silverware. The family's voices—joyous, raucous, thankful to be together—compete with the skeptical congregational voices I've imagined and shout "Amen!" to the voice of the psalmist. My father-in-law is rich: rich in relationships, memories, laughter, and love: "Thus is the man blessed who fears the Lord."

I jot down a provisional outline based on my conversation with the text:

> Gut reaction—skepticism.
> Proposed "solution"—cultural distance.
> Nagging question—are we really all that different?
> Family portrait—large family a blessing.
> Counter-cultural proposal—"Thus is the man blessed who fears the LORD."

I will not state these as "points" in the sermon; they're only meant to help me recall my experience of the text. Maybe I won't use the outline at all, if further reflection requires me to scrap it. Maybe I got off track with that "gut reaction" and I will decide that only a few exceptional people in my congregation are as skeptical as I imagined. Or, moving in a different direction, maybe I will decide that the answer to my "nagging question" is that the cultural divide between us and the psalm's first readers *is* a major factor, that times have changed, and now that more children survive infancy, the ideal number of childbirths is not what it used to be.

I have yet to grapple with "Jerusalem" (v. 5) and "Israel" (v. 6), and how they affect the application of this psalm to twenty-first century Christians. I have not yet invited biblical scholars or theologians to join my conversation with the text; maybe my commentaries will take me in a different direction altogether.

I need to let these other voices weigh in so that my handling of the text is not idiosyncratic. Too many flights of fancy pose as sermons, those who preach them justifying absurdity or even heresy because they will not discipline imagination with reason, Scripture, and tradition. But my point remains: an outline for a sermon on a psalm may well look something like the one I have sketched.

More than a traditional didactic outline, it respects the logic of poetry and experience.

Liturgical "Logic"

What holds a psalm together and makes sense of its movement may not be an individual's experience, whether the poet's or the preacher's, but corporate experience—corporate worship, for example.

In Psalm 69, for instance, the poet grinds the gears of complaint for twenty-nine verses. Then, without warning, he shifts to praise in verse 30, and the psalm coasts home in this mode. What accounts for this sudden shift? Some scholars posit a liturgical rationale for the abrupt transition from pain to praise in the lament psalms. Perhaps in the public performance of Psalm 69 a priest or liturgist interjected words of promise not included in the text, assuring petitioners that their complaint has been heard, their sin pardoned, their petition granted. This prompts the (apparent) sudden burst of praise.

Bernhard Anderson writes:

> This "abrupt change of mood" in the laments, to which Hermann Gunkel once called attention, is quite striking. It is doubtful whether it can be explained solely on the basis of the psalmist's inner certainty. It seems likely that the transition from sorrow to rejoicing, from lament to thanksgiving, was occasioned by something that occurred in the setting of worship within which these Psalms had their place. There is reason to believe that at a certain moment in the service a member of the Temple personnel, a priest or sometimes a prophet, pronounced an "oracle of salvation" which assured the suppliant of God's grace and favor. None of these "oracles" has been preserved, but now and then we find hints that they were spoken.[9]

Whether or not the reconstruction corresponds to actual practice

---

9 Bernhard W. Anderson, *Out of the Depths* (Westminster, 1983), 108.

in Israel's history,[10] surely the Christian preacher is in a position to speak the "priestly oracle":

> "If we confess our sins he is faithful and just to forgive us our sins."

> "What shall separate us from the love of Christ?"

> "In him all God's promises are 'Yes' and 'Amen.'"

> "I will never leave you or forsake you."

These assurances, rooted in the gospel and heralded by its ministers, enable the Christian to turn from lament to praise. Without sugar-coating the bitter pills of the lament psalms, without pretending that life is sweeter than it is, we can affirm that Christ has drained the wretched cup on our behalf and has graced us with authentic joy in a world gone sour.

A different sort of corporate worship experience lies behind Psalm 24.

> [1]The earth is the LORD's, and everything in it,
> the world, and all who live in it;
> [2]for he founded it upon the seas
> and established it upon the waters.

> [3]Who may ascend the hill of the LORD?
> Who may stand in his holy place?
> [4]He who has clean hands and a pure heart,
> who does not lift up his soul to an idol
> or swear by what is false.
> [5]He will receive blessing from the LORD

---

10 The form-critical hypothesis may be unnecessary. Dan Allender and Tremper Longman propose a credible "psychological" explanation for the psalmists' abrupt mood changes in *The Cry of the Soul* (NavPress, 1994), 245–259 J. Clinton McCann likewise sees no need for the "oracle of salvation" hypothesis, finding the psalmists' dual moods true to the believer's life of prayer: *A Theological Introduction to the Book of Psalms* (Abingdon, 1993), 96–97.

and vindication from God his Savior.
⁶Such is the generation of those who seek him,
    who seek your face, O God of Jacob.   *Selah*

⁷Lift up your heads, O you gates;
    be lifted up, you ancient doors,
    that the King of glory may come in.
⁸Who is this King of glory?
    The LORD strong and mighty,
    the LORD mighty in battle.
9Lift up your heads, O you gates;
    lift them up, you ancient doors,
    that the King of glory may come in.
¹⁰Who is this King of glory?
    The LORD Almighty—
    he is the King of glory.   *Selah*

This poem does not feature "logical" connections between its three stanzas. No "therefore," "yes, but," or other transitional words connect the three movements of this poem (vv. 1–2; 3–6; 7–10). At a glance, these movements may even appear disconnected, the transitions between them inexplicably abrupt. But when we realize the psalm is an entrance liturgy, the connecting thread becomes easy to trace. The first stanza reminds us that the God whose presence we invoke is incomparably great. Stanza two asks who is worthy to stand in the presence of this incomparably great One. Certainly not David, who fell short of every test he mentions in these lines. Certainly not you or me. Yet, amazingly, the third stanza invites us to welcome God into our presence anyway, to open the gates of our city, our church, our hearts, and let him in. How can this be? Because he is the "God of Jacob" (v. 6). *Jacob!* If God accepted that scoundrel, maybe there's hope for the rest of us!

    A sermon following this poem's logic will begin with a sense of God's awesome majesty. Next, the sermon will evoke a sense of unworthiness to be in God's presence: what temple, what church, what people presumes to serve as suitable habitation for the One who made and possesses all things? Lastly, the sermon will call the people of this gracious God to fling open the doors of their hearts "that the King of glory may come in." Ideally, this message would be preached early in the worship service, with congregational songs, prayers and offerings following as a natural response to God's Word preached (see strategy 13 in chapter 8).

Summary

The psalms do not open their treasures to preachers who insist on treating them like epistles or theological arguments. If we will follow the logic of poetry when shaping sermons on psalms, we will be more likely to capitalize on their inspired poemness and change how listeners think and feel when they hear this part of God's Word.

Strategy 4
Renarratize the Psalm

While it is true that the logic of poetry is not ordinarily the logic of narrative, "story-telling" can be a genre-sensitive method of preaching at least two kinds of psalms: historical psalms, and psalms based on someone's story.

Historical Psalms

Psalms 78, 105, 106, 136, and part of Psalm 135 recount some of the major events of Israel's story. God's people needed to hear again and again what he had done to constitute them as a privileged nation, so it is not surprising that several songs in their hymnal recall this redemptive history. God's people still need to hear the story— the old but ongoing story in which we find ourselves. These psalms make great preaching texts.

They do not really need to be *re*-narrated; the preacher simply fleshes out what the poet has sketched. Except that "simply" is probably not the right word here: these psalms can be tricky to preach. For one thing, they are long and cover a lot of ground. A sermon that tries to give a bird's eye view of many centuries may prove to be about as interesting as the time line in the back of a history text. The sermon's retelling needs to be selective and tightly crafted (as is the poet's) so that each episode is vivid even though recounted briefly.

And each episode of the sermon must further the poem's theological agenda. These psalms are not history for history's sake: they are *his*-story. God is the central and indispensable character in all of them.[11] His mighty acts were done in the past and are recounted in the present so that Israel might obey his law (especially Psalm 105; see v. 45), trust his mercy (especially Psalm 106, which recalls her faithlessness despite his commitment to them), and celebrate his steadfast love (especially Psalm 136 with its antiphonal response to each historical datum).

The preacher needs to let the agenda of these poems provide direction and coherence for sermons that might otherwise disintegrate into catalogs of dusty facts. One way to do this can be illustrated by Psalm 78. Here the poet uses several key linking words which should feature prominently in a sermon on this psalm: "but," "yet," "in spite of," and "again." Ordinarily, perhaps, a storyteller will not think too much about conjunctions; here, however, they are crucial. The whole point of the psalm is to contrast Israel's incorrigibility ("again and again they put God to the test") with God's amazing grace ("time after time he restrained his anger"). His grace is evident even in his judgments, which indicate that he was not going to give up on them. The sermon must say these key words at least as often as the text does. The preacher will want to punch them, not only when reading and commenting on the text, but when making application to contemporary listeners: "*In spite of* all that God has done for us . . . That close call should have cured me forever, *yet* again I . . . We confidently promise to serve him more faithfully from now on, *but* . . ."

The psalm's climax imagines God as waking from a drunken sleep (what a brash simile!) to try something new, something more effective than past efforts to discipline his wayward people. What

---

11 See Kenneth Langley, "Theocentric View," in *Homiletics and Hermeneutics: Four Views on Preaching Today*, ed. Scott M. Gibson and Matthew D. Kim (Baker Academic, 2018), 81–106.

will it be? What can succeed where past attempts have failed? David. He gave them David. Centuries later he gave us David's greater Son. The Anointed Shepherd-King is God's solution to his people's persistent waywardness then and now. The psalm and the sermon prepare us to hear at last this word of grace by repeating "but," "yet," "still," "even though," and "again and again" so that God's severe mercy is heard as almost too good to be true.

The historical psalms with their narrativity right there on the surface are few in number. But many psalms have a story below the surface. Some have notations linking them to episodes in David's career, signaling that they are meant to be read as in some sense commentary on those stories. Others were possibly prompted by the experience of the unnamed poet or of a group, even though no inscription tells us precisely what transpired and even though details in the poem itself may be sketchy. Somebody was in dire straits and was rescued. Somebody got sick and was healed. Somebody was taunted, exiled, betrayed. Somebody sinned. The poems may not tell these stories, but the stories gave birth to the poems. One potentially powerful way to preach these psalms is to retell those stories or others like them.

Recovering the Original Story

Almost half the psalms begin with the words "of David," which may signify Davidic authorship or sponsorship or inclusion in an earlier collection which had ties to David. Of these, fourteen are linked by their inscription to an occasion in David's life as recorded in the books of Samuel (Psalms 3, 7, 18, 30, 34, 51, 52, 54, 56, 57, 59, 60, 63, 142). Most scholars believe that the inscriptions are not original but were added by later hands to suggest that these poems can be fruitfully read against the background of the narratives.[12] To read Psalm 51, for example, as relating to the Bathsheba affair and

---

12 Any standard Old Testament introduction will summarize interpretive options for "of David." It is interesting that scholarship seems to be moving toward a more "conservative" stance, taking the Psalms-David connection seriously. See James L. Mays, "The David of the Psalms," chapter 9 in *The Lord Reigns: A Theological Handbook to the Psalms* (Westminster John Knox, 1994).

its aftermath, is to deepen our appreciation of the poem and how it applies to us even if our sin is not identical with David's, and even if David did not write it.

Whether or not David wrote Psalm 51, the inscription encourages us to read the poem as commentary on his experience and to read that experience as illumined by the psalm. Is this not permission to retell David's story in a sermon on the psalm? Or, for that matter, to use the psalm when preaching 2 Samuel 11 and 12? The "fit" between Psalm 51 and the Bathsheba affair is so plausible we might have made the connection even if no inscription linked them.

In other "David" psalms, the match between poem and narrative is surprising—none more so than that suggested by Psalm 34's inscription: "Of David. When he feigned insanity before Abimelech, who drove him away, and he left." Anyone who remembers what happened in 1 Samuel 21 will find it remarkable that this psalm should be considered commentary on that story. David's escape from the Philistines was accomplished by his own quick thinking and deception. God does not appear to be involved at all. We may be convinced, in fact, that no self-respecting God would want credit for such an embarrassing incident. Yet the poem recognizes God at work in, through, and in spite of David's conniving and duplicity. Re-narratizing this poem by recounting the less than flattering episode in David's career gives the preacher a great opportunity to reflect on a profound theology of divine-human interaction.

One of the most enjoyable series I've ever preached was a twelve month exploration of the life and psalms of David. Alternating between narrative and poetic texts made for a homiletically varied menu. Typically, when the series brought us to an incident in 1 or 2 Samuel which is linked to a Davidic psalm by the poem's inscription, we read that narrative in the worship service prior to my preaching the psalm. This freed me from having to tell the story at length in the sermon so I could major on the text of the poem itself. Of course, this is not the only way to handle the David poems. Shorter ones, especially, permit a fuller retelling of the story during the sermon. The story, then, becomes the interpretive key to what the poem meant and means. John Calvin's expositions of the Davidic psalms model how it can be done: he comments on the psalm verse by verse, dipping imaginatively into the Samuel narratives wherever David's experience might plausibly shed light on the poem.

Telling a New Story

I'm inclined to accept psalm inscriptions as original and historical, though I do not think it makes much difference either way when it comes to appropriating these poems for ourselves. On the one hand, if the inscriptions were added by people other than the poets, we can still trust divine providence in this canonical process and follow the urging of Spirit-led editors who want us to read these poems against the background of David's career. If the inscriptions were there from the beginning, it is still the case that the vast majority of psalms, including "David" psalms, lack any kind of situational notation. This omission assures us that not knowing the original stories is no handicap to making them our own.[13] Although stories gave birth to these poems, the poems do not recount the stories. Details are sketchy. These poems are general enough for almost any reader to see himself or herself in them. Their relevance to each generation does not depend on our ability to reconstruct the original life setting.[14]

A sermon on one of these texts might imaginatively reconstruct a story that makes good sense of the emotions, petitions, and hints of narrative found in the psalm. The narrative could be set in the tenth century before Christ, in the experience of Christ himself (Spurgeon does this masterfully in a sermon on Psalm 22),[15] or it could be set in a subsequent era. For example, a sermon on Psalm

---

13 Paul Scott Wilson advises preachers on what to make of the "titles" of psalms in "Reading the Psalms for Preaching," in *Performing the Psalms*, ed. Dave Bland and David Fleer (Chalice, 2005), 116–117.

14 In addition to Wilson's chapter, cited in the previous footnote, and Brueggemann's essay in the same volume, see McCann and Howell, *Preaching the Psalms,* 28–29. They cite Spurgeon's apt comments on the timeless applicability of the Psalter to suffering readers in every age.

15 Ibid.

46 might retell Martin Luther's story, how he desperately needed a refuge, how he found one in God, and how, reflecting on Psalm 46, he wrote "A Mighty Fortress." Naturally, the sermon would be followed by singing the hymn. Dietrich Bonhoeffer connected Psalm 74 (a lament over Babylon's devastation of Jerusalem) to Kristallnacht, the night the Nazis devastated Jewish communities. A sermon on Psalm 74 could make this poem more contemporary by retelling that dreadful story from 1938 as well as the original story.

Who else in church history—who else in our own time—has claimed and prayed our psalm text? Walter Brueggemann suggests we ask this question and let the answer supply some new inscriptions for psalms:

"For the Sunday when the rains came after months of drought"
     (Psalm 148)
"For the day after 9/11" (Psalm 46)
"The prayer of a woman whose son is caught in gang crossfire"
     (Psalm 88).[16]

We will not claim canonical status for our inscriptions, but preaching them like this is within the canonical tradition of narratizing these poems.

Many psalms imply a story that's repeated in every generation, including our own. For these, my preference would be to construct a contemporary narrative. Psalm 73, for example, is the testimony of a man who almost lost his faith when he envied the prosperity of the wicked. This could be the story of a Christian in any age.

John never really struggled much with doubt till he was fifty. In college his faith had been stretched by science courses and exposure to people of other religions. But it came through stronger for having been challenged. John was convinced that Christianity accounts for more of life than any alternative hypothesis and with fewer problems. God and God's word seemed a sure foundation on which to build a life.

16 "Psalms in Narrative Performance," in *Performing the Psalms*, ed. Bland and Fleer (Chalice, 2005), 21–23. I have adapted some of Brueggemann's suggestions.

*John loved this God and wanted to serve him. He earned a Mas-
ter's degree in Church Music and went on to serve three successive
congregations as a worship pastor. He loved his work. He loved his
gorgeous, godly wife, and their three kids, including their Downs
Syndrome child, Ryan. John took it pretty well when Ryan was born
handicapped. He knew that many people doubt God's goodness or
even God's existence when trouble comes their way. But John saw no
reason to doubt just because bad things happen to good people. Lately, however, his faith has taken a hit from a different angle: what if
good things happen to bad people?*

*John has to supplement his church income by playing in a local
orchestra and teaching private lessons. The extra money helps cover
Ryan's medical bills. The boy has already lived longer than expected,
placing enormous financial burdens on his family. This has taken its
toll on Judith, whose own health has suffered, and on their daughters' ability to attend good colleges; what money that might have
been available for education went instead to doctors and hospitals
and now to the residential facility where they reluctantly concluded
Ryan would get the kind of care they can no longer give.*

*All in all, God has surely been good to them. But, something has
been bugging John lately. The daughter of the cellist he plays with
in the orchestra is going to Julliard this fall. The conductor's son is
headed to Princeton. John knows he should be happy for these col-
leagues, but frankly, he's jealous. Neither of them cares for church or
God or morality, or anything—John thinks in his more cynical moments— except music and money.*

*If they were miserable in their godlessness, that would be one
thing, but they're two of the happiest people he knows. Everybody
likes them and wants to be around them. They work out at a pricey
fitness center. They take expensive vacations. They joke about John's
twelve-year-old Dodge that spends as much time in the shop as in
his driveway. And at last night's rehearsal, the cellist, a smug agnos-
tic, parked her brand-new Mustang next to John's clunker.*

*Driving a clunker he can accept (hey, it's "good stewardship").
Community college for his talented daughters he can accept. A low
salary he can accept. On a good day John can accept just about anything, even Downs Syndrome. But doggone it, the prosperity of these
vibrant people who flaunt their wealth and their tanned bodies and*

their kids' success and their agnosticism is starting to grate on him.

> *They have no struggles;*
>   *their bodies are healthy and strong.*
> *They are free from the burdens common to man;*
>   *they are not plagued by human ills.*
> *Therefore pride is their necklace;*
>   *they clothe themselves with violence.*
> *Oh yes, violence. Last week Audrey was laughing about her four*
>   *abortions.*

And so the re-narratizing of Psalm 73 begins. The rest of verses 4-11 will be heard, a counter-claim to the orthodox credo of the psalmist (and John), "Surely God is good to Israel, to those who are pure in heart" (v. 1). The preacher will expose John's subconscious self-pity, expressed in Asaph's words, "Surely in vain I have kept my heart pure." The congregation will learn that John came close to chucking his faith ("My feet had almost slipped"); that he almost went public with his doubts, but was later glad that something held him back ("If I had said, 'I will speak thus,' I would have betrayed this generation of your children"). I made the fictional John a minister to emphasize the potential damage if he voiced everything he was thinking.

But then, the story continues, something happened in church the following Sunday. John heard something, sang something, remembered something—and went home that day satisfied with God ("Earth has nothing I desire besides you"), even though the old clunker broke down and he had to walk the last mile and a half.

A sermon that takes this approach to a psalm will have to be careful that the story does not trump the text. It is the poem itself we are preaching; the story, should we choose to use one, is just a vehicle for delivering the poem. Furthermore, the story should not be about "John," but about God. He is the chief character in the biblical story and every part of that story. Keeping him central by naming him often and prominently will help keep the theological concern of the text and sermon from getting lost in the story.

For Further Study

Paul Scott Wilson discusses "fictive plot" as a paradigm for renar-ratizing psalms in "Reading the Psalms for Preaching," chapter 6 in *Performing the Psalms*, ed. Dave Bland and David Fleer (Chal-ice, 2005).

Talk about It

What dangers might there be in outlining our experience of the text instead of the text itself?

Dig Deeper

Scholars have proposed various theories for the abrupt change of mood in the lament psalms. Among these proposals are two that are quite different and might imply quite different homiletical ap-proaches: (1) the liturgical theory, that in the oral performance of the psalm an officiant spoke a word of promise or, perhaps, forgiveness (a word not preserved) in the text as we have it; and (2) the psychological theory, that in the act of lifting up a com-plaint to God the speaker came to a reassurance that God heard and that God would act. How might two sermons on the same lament psalm be different depending on which of these theories the preacher adopted?

Practice

Read a psalm, jotting down your impressions and feelings as you go (do not worry about exegetical precision or historical-gram-matical exegesis yet; you're after your experience of the text as a work of art). Now reflect on what you've written: does it have po-tential as an outline that would enable others to experience what you did as you read?

4

Poetics

Poetry, working through a complex sys-
tem of linkages of sound, image, word,
rhythm, syntax, theme, ideas, is an in-
strument for conveying densely patterned
meanings . . . that are not readily convey-
able through other kinds of discourse.[1]
Robert Alter

A poem should not mean
But be.[2]
Archibald MacLeish

Defining poetry, like nailing Jell-O to the wall, is a slippery job.
Dictionaries disagree. Anthology editors hem and haw. Poets
themselves offer quasi-definitions like "the best words in the best
order" (Coleridge) or "the desirable gooseflesh which is poetry"
(Dickinson). Most preachers will probably have to settle for saying, like the Supreme Court justice defining pornography, "I recognize it when I see it."

We recognize it when we see it in the Bible because publishers
print it in lines instead of paragraphs. We recognize it in the Psalter because we find musical notations in the text. And because its
language is more densely packed than ordinary speech, its use of

---

1 Robert Alter, *The Art of Biblical Poetry* (Basic Books, 1985), 113,
2 Archibald MacLeish, "Ars Poetica" from *Collected Poems 1917–1982* (Houghton Mifflin, 1985), 106.

imagery more pervasive, its lines parallel in structure, its sound, its feel somehow different. Getting more specific about the "somehow" is what's slippery.[3]

But no matter. We're not editors at Merriam Webster, we're preachers. It is enough to know that poetry differs from prose and to develop a feel for this difference even if we struggle to express it in words. It is enough to know, for instance, that poetry does not major in propositions. The psalmists believed truth about God, and this truth can be expressed propositionally; but that's not how they chose to express it. For these poets, propositional content is not the only part, and maybe not the most important part of the poetic package. We dishonor their work and cheat our listeners if we shrivel these living poems down to dry facts like old raisins under the car seat.

What's more, we dishonor the Spirit who inscripturated truth in the psalms if all we do is rummage through his poetry for its paraphraseable content. Respect for *how* these poems mean demands that we preach them differently. Here, then, are some homiletical strategies under the slippery rubric, "poetics," the study of how poetry works.

Strategy 5
Use Poetic Devices to Recreate the Psalm's Rhetorical Effects

Psalmists use parallelism and puns, anaphora and assonance, alliteration, acrostics, chiasm, and other devices for dramatic effect and delight, to surprise and sustain interest, to stir emotion and aid memory, and to say a lot with a little.

Can we recapture the rhetorical effects of these devices by using

---

3 Some scholars question whether "poetry" and "prose" are helpful rubrics for biblical literature. Kugel, for instance, doubts that the differences between alleged poems and prose in the Hebrew Bible amount to much; *The Idea of Biblical Poetry* (Yale University Press, 1981). Others, like Watson, Fokkelman, Alter, Peterson and Richards concede that Kugel sounds some important cautionary notes, but believe that differences, though undoubtedly a matter of degree, are significant enough to merit a distinction between the two broad genres of literature in the Bible.

them in sermons on the psalms? Exact duplication of a psalm's effect on its original audience is, of course, impossible. The rhetorical situation of the preacher and congregation in a new time and place differs from that of a psalm's first hearers. And a sermon differs from a poem or song; however much the preacher may try to respect the rhetorical and poetic dynamics of the psalm genre, the sermon is its own genre. Furthermore, some features of Hebrew poetry do not carry over into English.

Still, the way a poem works might clue the preacher into the way a sermon on that poem could work. Some features of the original composition *do* survive translation: refrain, for instance. What use might the preacher make of this device? Or if the poem features chiasm, what might that pattern suggest about the focus and flow of the sermon? Even devices which are lost in translation can be pointed out as part of a genre-sensitive explication of the psalm, helping those who do not read Hebrew to appreciate the aesthetics of the text. Depending on the preacher's own poetic flair, English poetic devices might be brought into the service of the Word, giving the sermon a poetic feel that approximates that of the original.

Hebrew Poetic Devices that Survive Translation

Refrain

Refrains occur in Psalms 39, 42, 43, 44, 46, 49, 56, 57, 59, 62, 67, 78, 80, 99, 107, 118, 134, 144, and 145. They range from the extreme (some would say monotonous) repetition of "His love endures forever" twenty-six times in Psalm 136, to the subtle yet significant variations on the refrains of Psalm 49:12 and 20, and Psalm 59:9 and 17. In these two psalms, an earlier thought is echoed at the end, but with a twist, thanks to new insight provided by the development of the poem:

> O my Strength, I watch for you;
>> you, O God, are my fortress, my loving God. (59:9)
> O my Strength, I sing praise to you;
>> you, O God, are my fortress, my loving God. (59:17)

The change in Psalm 59's refrain is slight, but significant. In the first instance, when the poet affirms God as his Strength, he is watchful, hopeful, looking for help in distress. By the end of the poem, however, when the refrain is repeated, he's so confident that his petition will be heard and heeded, he's able to replace "watch" with "praise."

The alteration in Psalm 49's refrain is even greater:[4]

> But man, despite his riches, does not endure;
>   he is like the beasts that perish. (49:12)
> A man who has riches without understanding
>   is like the beasts that perish. (49:20)

In this wisdom psalm, the poet-sage observes that humans are "like the beasts that perish." But the refrain in verse 20, following as it does the psalmist's reflections on this theme, clarifies that it's the person *who has riches without understanding* who is like the beasts that perish. The refrain means more than it did at first pass. A sermon on this text could repeat the key line several times (like Qoheleth did with "vanity, vanity"), but then conclude with the fuller significance of the refrain in its altered form.

Sometimes a refrain marks stanzaic divisions, or expresses the main idea of a poem, or brings closure to the piece, or does all of the above, as in Psalm 46:

> [1] God is our refuge and strength,
>   an ever present help in trouble.
> [2] Therefore we will not fear, though the earth give way
>   and the mountains fall into the heart of the sea,
> [3] though its waters roar and foam
>   and the mountains quake with their surging.   *Selah*
> [4] There is a river whose streams make glad the city of God
>   the holy place, where the Most High dwells.
> [5] God is within her, she will not fall;

---

4 The difference in wording between these two verses is lost in the LXX and Syriac, both of which give identical readings for Psalm 49:12 and 20. My discussion here assumes the Hebrew reading and NIV translation.

God will help her at break of day.
⁶ Nations are in uproar, kingdoms fall;
   he lifts his voice, the earth melts.
⁷ The LORD Almighty is with us;
   the God of Jacob is our fortress.   *Selah*

⁸ Come and see the works of the LORD,
   the desolations he has brought upon the earth.
⁹ He makes wars cease to the ends of the earth;
   he breaks the bow and shatters the spear,
   he burns the shields with fire.
¹⁰ "Be still, and know that I am God;
   I will be exalted among the nations,
   I will be exalted in the earth."

¹¹ The LORD Almighty is with us;
   the God of Jacob is our fortress.   *Selah*

The refrain in verse 7 concludes the first stanza, marks the center of the poem, and presses home its central claim, "The LORD Almighty is with us; the God of Jacob is our fortress." Verse 11 repeats these words, wrapping up this short psalm in an aesthetically satisfying way. A sermon faithful to the text will not ignore this key feature of Psalm 46: it will have two movements, punctuated by the refrain. Perhaps the preacher will milk the fortress metaphor and repeat the refrain often enough and effectively enough that members of the congregation will remember it all week long.

"Why so downcast, O my soul?" the refrain that ties Psalms 42 and 43 together, invites hearers to hold a thoughtful conversation with themselves and talk themselves out of spiritual depression.⁵ Repeating and expounding on this refrain in a sermon extends that invitation to a new generation of hearers and makes it difficult to hear the psalm without making some kind of personal response.

Absence of a refrain may be homiletically significant. Psalm

5 See Martin Lloyd-Jones's exposition of these Psalms in *Spiritual Depression* (Eerdmans, 1965), 9–21.

107 sketches five scenarios of distress. The first four end with the words, "Let them give thanks to the Lord for his unfailing love and his wonderful deeds for men" (vv. 8, 15, 21, and 31), plus an additional line tailored to the situation of distress from which God had provided deliverance. Naturally, we expect to hear these words again after the fifth vignette, but they are not there. Verses 32–43, like the preceding stanzas, describe a group of needy but now rescued people who have reason to praise the Lord. Only this time the expected refrain is missing. Some scholars think that the refrain may have been dropped accidentally by copyists. Although this is *possible*, there is no way to be certain. The preacher will ask what is the rhetorical effect of the refrain's absence in the poem as we have it, and work with that. In the case of Psalm 107, the absence of a refrain invites listeners to supply one for themselves, thus participating in the poem more actively.

So a preacher might punctuate a sermon on this psalm with the refrain: "Let *us* give thanks to the Lord" but, like the poet, leave it off at the end. If the conclusion is worded and delivered just right, the congregation will feel the need to complete the sermon for themselves, silently mouthing the refrain one last time. Or maybe the preacher will lead them in doing so out loud.

Similarly, the refrain of Psalm 62:2 and 6 ("He alone is my rock and my salvation; he is my fortress, I will not be shaken") does not appear in verse 12 at the end of the poem, where we might expect to find it again. A sermon on this psalm could end with the congregation speaking the refrain, or singing a contemporary praise song based on it, bringing both sermon and service to an aesthetically and emotionally satisfying conclusion.

Other kinds of repetition occur in the psalms: *inclusio*, beginning and ending the poem with the same word or motif (Psalms 8, 118, 136, and the "Halleluiah" psalms 146–150); *apostrophe*, as in Psalms 115:9–11 and 118:2–4, with the only variation being the names inserted in the repeated phrase; *anaphora*, in which a key word or phrase is repeated with incremental advance in thought with each repetition (the "How many?" of Psalm 3 and the "How long?" of Psalm 13); and *echo*, as in Psalm 130:6, with its plaintive line:

My soul waits for the LORD
   more than watchmen wait for the morning,
   more than watchmen wait for the morning.

Preachers who encounter these forms of repetition in the psalms will want to ask, "Why is this repeated? What is its rhetorical effect? Might I use this to recreate its affective, imaginative, aesthetic impact?"[6] As Thomas Long does in his proposed handling of Psalm 19:7–10:

> The psalmist employs the technique of parallelism to praise the torah, the central teaching of the faith. The verses come at us like measured drum beats: "the *law* of the Lord," "the *testimony* of the Lord," "the *precepts* of the Lord," "the *commandments* of the Lord." These terms are almost but not quite synonymous. Each describes the Torah, but each construes it in its own way, and with special virtue and benefit: "perfect, reviving the soul," "sure, making wise the simple," "right, rejoicing the heart," "pure, enlightening the eyes." The movement of the text, then, is march-like in cadence and advance, and its rhetorical impact is to invite the reader to fall in step.[7]

This psalm, therefore, provides the opportunity to create a sermon that does more than name the many ways by which we describe the truth of the faith (e.g., law; gospel; testimony; good news; teachings of the faith; old, old story). It not only fleshes out the power of that truth in our lives (e.g., revives our souls; renews our hopes; turns our foolishness into wisdom; creates joy; opens our eyes to human need) but also marches in rhythmic drumbeat fashion, inviting the hearer to join in the march. Instead of, "The third thing I want to say about the truth of the Christian faith," the congregation would hear a series of similar

---

6 Edward P. J. Corbett notes that certain figures of speech (forms "artfully varied from common usage") are calculated to work directly on the emotions. *Classical Rhetoric for the Modern Student*, 3rd ed. (Oxford University Press, 1990), 425.

7 Thomas G. Long, *Preaching and the Literary Forms of the Bible* (Fortress, 1989), 131–132.

refrains punctuating the movements of the sermon: "The law of the Lord is perfect, reviving the soul." "The good news of the gospel is sure, renewing our hope." "The old, old story of God's way with the world is true, calling us to justice."[8]

Chiasm

Chiasm, too, carries over into English translation, and can be a homiletically fruitful poetic device. In this crossing structure the second half of a poetic unit echoes the first by repeating key words or motifs in reverse order: ABC/C'B'A'. Sometimes an unrepeated element stands at the middle: ABC/D/C'B'A'.

Chiasm appears so frequently in the psalms that it appears to have been used quite naturally if not unconsciously by the Hebrew poets. It is found within the parallel cola of hundreds of individual lines, as in Psalm 145:2.

A Every day
   B I will praise you
   B' and extol your name
A' for ever and ever.

But more important for preachers are those chiasms which shape entire psalms. Robert Alden, who found chiastic structure in about a third of the psalms, offered the clear example of Psalm 8:

A Benediction (v.1)
   B God's rule (vv. 2–3)
      C Man's meanness (v. 4)
      C' Man's greatness (v. 5)
   B' Man's rule (vv. 6–8)
A' Benediction (v. 9)[9]

---

8 Ibid.

9 Robert L, Alden, "Chiastic Psalms: A Study in the Mechanics of Semitic Poetry," *Journal of the Evangelical Theological Society* 17, no. 1 (1974): 11–28. Two additional articles continued Alden's investigation of chiastic Psalms: *Journal of*

Chiasm supplies the preacher with an interpretive clue because the poem's central claim appears at the middle point. Occasionally it will also suggest a homiletical clue because the sermon can follow the chiastic movement of the text. In Psalm 67, for example, we find this structure: two lines / refrain / one line / refrain / two lines:

¹ May God be gracious to us and bless us
   and make his face shine upon us,   *Selah*
² that your ways may be known on earth,
   your salvation among all the nations.

³ May the peoples praise you, O God;
   may all the peoples praise you.

⁴ May the nations be glad and sing for joy,
   for you rule the peoples justly
   and guide the nations of the earth.   *Selah*
⁵ May the peoples praise you, O God;
   may all the peoples praise you.

⁶ Then the land will yield its harvest,
   and God, our God, will bless us.
⁷ God will bless us,
   and all the ends of the earth will fear him.

The structure of this poem is apparent:

A May God bless us (vv. 1–2)
   B Refrain (v. 3)
      C The nations rejoice in God (v. 4)
   B' Refrain (v. 5)
A' God will bless us (vv. 6–7)

the *Evangelical Theological Society* 19, no. 3 (1976): 191–200; and *Journal of the Evangelical Theological Society* 21, no. 3 (1978): 199–210.

"Earth" appears in both the first and last sections of the poem (translated "land" in v. 6, NIV), as does "the nations" (translated "ends of the earth" in v. 7). "Earth" also appears in the central line:

> May the nations be glad and sing for joy,
>> for you rule the peoples justly
>> and guide the nations of the earth.

The psalmist has pulled out every poetic trick in the book to focus our attention on the longest line in the psalm. It is bounded before and after by a refrain, followed by "Selah," and sits at the center of the chiasm. Here we have the ancient equivalent of a line printed in a different font, all caps, bold, and twice as large as everything else on the page. It is hard to miss the poem's thematic center, a prayer that all the nations of the earth sing for joy to their Sovereign.

But it is still possible to miss: more than one commentator has called the petition of verse 1 the theme of the poem—the petition that God bless "us." But although this is where the psalm begins, the chiastic structure shows that the poet's vision extends beyond "us," beyond the borders of Israel to encompass the Gentile nations. "Peoples" (or "nations") appears in every measure, or colon, from verse three through verse five—the refrains and the long central line.

A preacher seeking to make faithful use of this poetic device might begin a sermon talking about the American church's longing for God's blessing: we want him to prosper our congregations, our publishing houses, our parochial schools, our denominations, our families and political initiatives. But the psalm's vision, focused through its form, compels the sermon to look beyond our prosperity to our mission. The church is God's people *for others*. God's favor toward us is inextricably tied to our being a blessing to the nations. To the extent that we fulfill that mission, both psalm and sermon conclude, we will enjoy the smile of divine approval. The chiastic structure of both psalm and sermon underscores the great missional heart of the Bible. The welfare of God's chosen people, which we long for and which he is eager to grant, is both instrument and result of his being known and praised by the nations.

Poetic Devices that Do Not Carry over into English

These suggestions for using refrain and chiasm represent just a few of the homiletical possibilities for shaping sermons by the Psalter's poetics. Other devices used by the psalmists may likewise prove suggestive for preachers who want sermons to work in a way that is compatible with how the original compositions worked.

What about poetic features that do not translate well into English: gender parallelism, alliteration, rhythm, assonance or consonance, word play of various kinds, acrostics, and onomatopoeia, to name a few? Must the preacher simply ignore them when shaping the sermon? Maybe. It depends not only on whether the poetic device can be "translated," but also on what use the poet made of it. Some acrostics, for example, were probably intended mainly as memory aids. Since we are not trying to get listeners to memorize these psalms (not a bad idea, though), the acrostic pattern will probably not feature prominently in the sermon.

But what if the acrostic structure of the psalm is part of its meaning? Psalm 119 is an elaborately constructed acrostic poem, the first lines of every stanza (each eight lines long) beginning with successive letters of the Hebrew alphabet. All but two of its 176 verses include synonyms for Torah: statute, commandment, precept, and so on. It's almost as if eight rabbis were having coffee when someone suggested that, just for fun, they see how many aphorisms about Torah they could come up with, working their way through the alphabet.

We may not know how this psalm came to be composed, but there's no doubt about the effect of its structure. Psalm 119, in what it says and *how* it says it, asserts the sufficiency and applicability of God's Word for all of life from A to Z. God's testimonies, God's laws, God's statutes, precepts, decrees, and commands address every human need and every situation. "The Scriptures are the comprehensive equipment of the man of God and fit him fully for all branches of his work" (2 Tim 3:17, Phillips New Testament). Such God-ordained adequacy is trumpeted by Psalm 119's content *and form.*

How can a sermon's form make the same claim? Maybe the preacher could illustrate the wisdom and winsomeness of a Torah-oriented life by vignettes from birth to death, punctuated by verses from this psalm. Or preach an alphabetically outlined sermon on the ABCs of Torah-keeping. In one way or another, the claim sounded in the psalm's structure should be echoed by the sermon's structure.

English Poetic Devices

The psalmists' tools may not serve for our linguistically and culturally distant generation. Preachers may need to find alternative ways to achieve what the psalmists sought to achieve. Does a psalm's terseness or ellipsis create intentional ambiguity? We might accomplish that effect by vocal inflection. Does the psalm make an allusion which was instantly familiar to its first hearers, but which is lost on our generation? The sermon might need a story or word picture that resurrects the referent for the congregation. Did the poet use chiasm mainly as a memory aid? We might use alliteration to achieve the same end. (But no forced alliteration, please! Too many texts are forced to say what they do not say because a preacher needs another "P.")

Perhaps some of the poem's features were meant mainly to convey aesthetic pleasure. If so, how can the preacher communicate the beauty of the text and of the biblical vision of life? Maybe through assonance or consonance, rhythm or rhyme, or other stylistic devices that give the sermon a poetic sound? How about a striking phrase, like Ron Mehl's, "God works the night shift," for Psalm 121,[10] or Clovis Chappell's, "The Transience of Tears" for Psalm 30:5.[11] Or maybe instead of substituting an English poetic device, the poet's intended effect can be achieved through a cadenced delivery like that often heard in African-American preaching. Can the preacher find *some* way to give a sermon on a psalm a bit of poetic flair?

---

10 The title of Ron Mehl's book, *God Works the Night Shift* (Multnomah, 1994).

11 Clovis Chappell, *Sermons from the Psalms* (Abingdon, 1941), 141.

Be sure the device fits the poem. One student trying to be poetic in preaching his psalm text asked the class to imagine a series of scenes corresponding to sections of the psalm. I could tell he worked hard at painting word pictures for the various "stops" along the way. But the "journey motif" was foreign to the poem (there was no sense of geographic or narrative movement in the text). I applauded his willingness to experiment with an imaginative sermon form, but it didn't really work.

Seasoned preachers can make the same kind of mistake. I heard a respected Old Testament scholar preach on Psalm 73, using the image of a ladder to give the sermon coherence. The psalmist's progress from doubt to faith was likened to climbing the ladder; the movements of the sermon were steps up this ladder. That image may work with some texts, but not with this one. The poet testifies not to a series of incremental steps toward confident faith, but to an all-at-once "aha" moment when he entered the sanctuary of God and came to understand the final destiny of the wicked.

A meat and potatoes preacher might wonder, "Why work so hard at spicing up sermons on psalms?" The answer, of course, is that the devices and artistry of biblical poems are not mere spice, but an indispensable part of the God-breathed experience the poem delivers. "If the message were all that mattered in the Bible, we would be left wondering whether the biblical poets did not have anything better to do with their time than putting their utterances into the form of poetic parallelism and inventing apt metaphors. Biblical example leads us to conclude that in God's economy they did not have something better to do than to be artistic to the glory of God."[12]

For the glory of God, then, and not to draw attention to ourselves or to be admired for our homiletical virtuosity, preachers will try to respect and recreate how the poem means as well as what it means. Using the psalmist's poetic devices or English substitutes to accomplish similar rhetorical effects is one way to do this. Explication is another.

---

12 Leland Ryken, *Triumph of the Imagination* (InterVaristy, 1979), 41.

Strategy 6
Explicate the Poem

Explicate? Is not that what jaded graduate assistants do in English 101—dissect poems, lay the pieces out on the table to dry, and make students stare at them till they decide they can't stand poetry? There's a scene in the movie "Dead Poet's Society" where a literature teacher (played by Robin Williams) reads his class a deathly-dull explanation of poetry, then rips the page out of the textbook, shouting "Excrement!" Explication—is that any way to treat a psalm?

Anyone who has read a commentary by Derek Kidner or heard Kenneth Bailey exegete a Lukan parable has experienced the power of an exemplary explication. Anyone who has followed Robert Alter through a close reading of a biblical poem or Leland Ryken on a guided tour of a psalm knows that explication need not be boring: it can be one way to bring forth treasures old and new from a biblical poem.

To examine how the parts of a poem work in harmony, to help listeners notice creative artistry in a composition, to call attention to unusual word choice or harmonies of speech not apparent in translation, to demonstrate the fit between sound and sense in a poem—to do an explication, in other words—might be an effective way to illumine a text so that hearers see both what it means and how it means. Let's face it, poetry makes greater demands on readers than prose. Leading the congregation through a close reading of a psalm may help them experience its cognitive contents and its aesthetic shape.

One young Christian I know says he used to think Psalm 119 was incredibly monotonous. When reading through the Bible, he would skip it—that and the genealogies. Then one day he heard an explication of the psalm that demonstrated what the poem is doing through its acrostic structure, and he began to respect this masterpiece. I wonder how many other psalms could come alive for congregants if preachers would crack open these literary gems for them.

Explication as Part of a Sermon

Although a preacher might occasionally structure an entire sermon as an explication, more often explication will come in bits and pieces in a sermon whose over-all structure follows some other organizing principle. A sermon on Psalm 1, for instance, though it shapes itself around the contrasting images of tree and chaff, might also explain the walk/stand/sit motif of verse 1 or the chiasm naming "the wicked" in the first and last lines. A sermon on Psalm 73, though it shapes itself into three movements cued by the thrice-repeated "surely" in verses 1, 13, and 18, could also explicate the significant repetition of "slippage" ("my feet had almost slipped," v. 2, and "you place them on slippery ground," v. 18), or other details in this marvelous piece of literary art.

Psalm 8 illustrates how explication of literary features not only enhances aesthetic appreciation, but enables listeners to understand the theology of the poem.[13]

> [1] O LORD, our Lord,
> how majestic is your name in all the earth!
>
> You have set your glory
> above the heavens.
> [2] From the lips of children and infants
> you have ordained praise
> because of your enemies,
> to silence the foe and the avenger.
>
> [3] When I consider your heavens,
> the work of your fingers,
> the moon and the stars,
> which you have set in place,
> [4] what is man that you are mindful of him,
> the son of man that you care for him?

---

13 I am indebted to J. Clinton McCann for pointing out some of the features of Psalm 8 and their significance for preaching: *A Theological Introduction to the Book of Psalms* (Abingdon, 1993), 57–60.

⁵ You made him a little lower than the heavenly beings
   and crowned him with glory and honor.

⁶ You made him ruler over the works of your hands;
   you put everything under his feet:
⁷ all flocks and herds,
   and beasts of the field,
⁸ the birds of the air,
   and the fish of the sea,
   all that swim the paths of the seas.

⁹ O Lord, our Lord,
   how majestic is your name in all the earth!

An explication of this psalm's aesthetically pleasing chiasm and refrain will demonstrate that these devices mark theological as well
as literary boundaries. The poet acknowledges the majesty of man
as vice-regent over creation, but the starting and ending point of
any discussion of human authority must be that it is *derived* authority. Human glory and honor may stand at the thematic center
of the psalm, but they are bounded by the incomparable majesty
and sovereignty of our Maker.

Another noteworthy feature of the poem is the repetition
of "all" in verses 1, 6, 7, and 9 (NIV, "everything" in v. 6). This
key word stresses humanity's all-encompassing responsibility for
God's good earth. The recurring "all" in the middle of the poem
creates a sense of awesome but humbling accountability and prepares us to hear again the refrain in verse 9, where "*all* the earth" is
the arena of God's glory.

A faithful explication of this poem in the twenty-first century will help Christians honor the environmental concern of this
text, a concern that can only be treated in a biblically balanced
way by paying attention to the poem's literary features. If we notice only human dominion we will lean toward selfish misman-
agement of our fragile planet ("God put us in charge, we can do
as we please"). If we see only divine sovereignty we will lean toward complacency ("It's God's world, let him clean it up"). If we

advocate environmental responsibility divorced from worship of
the infinite personal God, we may unintentionally promote a kind
of New Age nature reverence all too common among those whose
care for the planet puts many Christians to shame but which tends
toward pantheism. But if we attend to the literary dimensions of
the text we can avoid these dangerous misreadings. What Robert
Alter says of readers goes for preachers as well:

> For a reader to attend to these elements of literary art is not
> merely an exercise in "appreciation" but a discipline of under-
> standing: the literary vehicle is so much the necessary medi-
> um through which the Hebrew writers realize their meanings
> that we will grasp the meanings at best imperfectly if we ignore
> their fine articulations as literature.[14]

I want my congregation to appreciate the Bible's artistry; after
all, the psalmists worked hard at crafting beautiful literature, and
explication is one way to honor their efforts. But even if I were
willing to leave aesthetic concerns aside, I would have to take the
literary features of psalm texts seriously because I want listeners to
see where the sermon's ideas come from. If I preach on environmental stewardship from Psalm 8 without some kind of explication similar to what I've sketched in the preceding paragraphs, the
congregation may or may not see that the sermon's case for both
divine sovereignty and human responsibility is rooted in the text.
They might think I'm just voicing my own opinions and using the
psalm as a convenient platform.

What to Say about a Poem

What else might a psalm explication include? How can a preacher
employ this genre-sensitive strategy?

---

14 Robert Alter, *The World of Biblical Literature* (Harper Collins, 1992), 63–
64. See also Patrick Miller, *Interpreting the Psalms* (Fortress, 1986), 30.

Call Attention to Poetic Devices

An explication might call attention to any of the poetic devices mentioned under the previous homiletical strategy—not, as there, to structure an entire sermon around them, but to point them out so that listeners notice and appreciate them. The chiasm of Psalm 67 is so important I might shape my whole sermon around it; but the chiasm of Psalm 1 is just one of several literary devices that may be worth pointing out so listeners can admire the artistry of the piece and the interplay of structure and theology. The refrain of Psalm 8 is so theologically significant I might structure my sermon by it; but the refrain in other psalms may be just one of several features worth a little bit of air time.

Unpack the Poet's Imagery

Here, again, there is overlap with a previous chapter. A preacher may on occasion grow an entire sermon from the psalm's imagery or speak in its word pictures; but in an explication, imagery does not feature quite so prominently or function in quite the same way. But it is not ignored, either. Can listeners understand Psalms 18, 89, 92, 98, 112, 132, and 148 without knowing what a "horn" is? An explication illumines this image of strength.

Is the hand in Psalm 123 poised to strike or to comfort and dispense gifts?

> As the eyes of slaves look to the hand of their master,
>> as the eyes of a maid look to the hand of her mistress,
> so our eyes look to the LORD our God,
>> till he shows us his mercy.

Some poems indulge in deliberate ambiguity, allowing readers to consider more than one possible reading.[15] But this psalm is not one of them; we have to make a choice about the correct interpretation of this image.

---

15 See Paul R. Raabe, "Deliberate Ambiguity in the Psalter," *Journal of Biblical Literature* 110 (1991): 213–227.

Leland Ryken counsels preachers to develop the poem's imagery before trying to explain or apply it.[16] *Picture* the horns on the ox. *Envision* the raised hand of the master or mistress. Do not be in a hurry to move on from the image of God as fortress to abstractions about "security" and "protection." First help listeners see the strong tower and sense the relief of hearing its gate clang shut after they are safe inside.

Like English poetry, psalms sometimes pass abruptly from one image to the next, trusting readers to make the connecting links.[17] Like English poetry, psalms vary in the types of imagery employed. Some images are at the same time profound symbols: Leviathan in Psalm 74, Rahab in Psalm 89, the Valley of Baca in Psalm 84. These symbols bear theological and imaginative freight, and a skillful explication will carry that weight over into the sermon.

Elucidate Figures of Speech

Figures of speech and imagery overlap, but are not identical. A figure of speech is a way of saying one thing while meaning another. It may or may not involve the language of sense experience, which is the essence of imagery. A few lines from Psalm 98 illustrate the difference.

- Verse 3 uses hyperbole, a *figure of speech*: "... all the nations of the earth have seen the salvation of our God."
- Verses 5 and 6 employ *aural imagery*: we hear harp, trumpet, horn, and song. These sounds are not figurative, but literal as our imaginations recreate them.
- Verse 8 features *both* imagery and figurative language. Again we hear sounds of praise, but now it is not literal; it is rivers clapping their hands and mountains singing.

The Psalms teem with figures of speech: *personification* (114:3–4), *apostrophe* (114:5), *simile* (1:3), *overstatement* (22:17),

---

16 Leland Ryken, "Metaphor in the Psalms," *Christianity and Literature* 21, no. 3 (1982): 13–19.

17 C.S. Lewis, *Reflections on the Psalms* (Harcourt, 1958), 63.

understatement (51:17), *metonymy,* a word standing for something
else ("May he send you help from the sanctuary and grant you support from Zion," Psalm 20:2, where "sanctuary' and "Zion" refer
to God's heavenly throne), and *synecdoche,* a variety of metonymy where a part stands for the whole ("May the foot of the proud
not come against me," 36:11). To these few examples we could add
dozens more. Rhetoricians have named as many as two hundred
and fifty figures of speech, many of which appear in the Bible.[18]
The preacher is not so much concerned to name them accurately
as to construe them correctly. Sometimes this will involve calling
attention to them in a sermonic explication.

One possible result? Aesthetic pleasure. In Molier's play, Mon-
sieur Jourdain is delighted to learn he's been speaking prose all his
life. Some who hear our sermons on the psalms may be delighted
to learn they've been reading figures of speech all their life, and
this delight is surely one of the Spirit's gifts to those who treasure
the Bible.

But there is more than aesthetic pleasure at stake. All the figures
mentioned above make listeners active partners in appropriating
meaning rather than passive recipients of meaning.[19] Striking language can tease the mind into fresh insight. Preachers who help
listeners notice and enjoy the power of non-literal language in this
psalm become instruments of the Holy Spirit in letting these poems do their life-changing work in hearts.[20]

Discuss the Mood or Tone of the Poem

Another way to explicate a poem is to unpack the emotion of the
text. "How do we feel when reading this psalm? Do you see how
the poet accomplishes this emotional effect?" We might call attention to the emotive connotations of words the poet chose from

---

18 As Bullinger's exhaustive study shows. E. W. Bullinger, *Figures of Speech
Used in the Bible* (Eyre and Spottiswood, 1898; reprinted by Baker, 1968).

19 Ryken, "Metaphor in the Psalms," 22–23.

20 What Leland Ryken said about scholarly exposition of the Psalms is true
of preaching the Psalms: "Taking the obligations of metaphor and simile seriously would revolutionize commentary on biblical poetry" (*Words of Delight* [Baker,
1992], 168).

among possible synonyms. We might note how the repetition of "How many" (Ps 3), "How long?" (Ps 13), or "My soul waits for the morning" (Ps 130) contributes not additional information but emotional color. We might note how in some laments poets rage, while in others they weep, and in others still they are too numb to feel much of anything. We might observe the effect of the poet's arrangement of source material: commenting on one section of Psalm 143, a preacher said, ". . . parts of previous psalms are placed here like a beautiful mosaic. They are arranged and edited as to make the appeal more earnest and also more beautiful. It is like a collection of different gems in a jeweler's window, each one sparkles with its individual brilliancy yet all are required to make the correct impression."[21]

Note the Adaptation of Sound to Sense

Alexander Pope believed that in poetry "the sound must seem an echo to the sense." The "what" of meaning and the "how" of meaning must fit. Where biblical poets have achieved this fit, preachers can let listeners in on the delight. A few examples:

- The antiphonal response expected in some psalms reminds us of their setting in corporate worship.
- The use of a "chorus" in Psalm 24 to ask "Who is this King of Glory?" not once but twice, heightens the pomp and drama of the poem.
- The catalog of creatures in Psalm 48, named in rapid succession, without pause for comment, fits the elegant simplicity of the poem's invitation for all creation to praise the Lord.
- The brevity of Psalm 117 underscores the urgency of its claim—that every person on earth ought to praise the Lord— as does the inclusion of his sacred name or pronoun in each of the five cola in this "little giant" of the Psalter.

For a slightly more developed example of fine fit between sound and sense, consider Psalm 29.

---

21 Calvin P. Swank, *Sermons from the Psalms* (Baker, 1962), 110.

¹Ascribe to the Lord, O mighty ones,
    ascribe to the Lord glory and strength.
²Ascribe to the Lord the glory due his name;
    worship the Lord in the splendor of his holiness.
³The voice of the Lord is over the waters;
    the God of glory thunders,
    the Lord thunders over the mighty waters.
⁴The voice of the Lord is powerful;
    the voice of the Lord is majestic.
⁵The voice of the Lord breaks the cedars;
    the Lord breaks in pieces the cedars of Lebanon.
⁶He makes Lebanon skip like a calf,
    Sirion like a young wild ox.
⁷The voice of the Lord strikes
    with flashes of lightning.
⁸The voice of the Lord shakes the desert;
    the Lord shakes the Desert of Kadesh.
⁹The voice of the Lord twists the oaks
    and strips the forests bare.
And in his temple all cry, "Glory!"

¹⁰The Lord sits enthroned over the flood;
    the Lord is enthroned as King forever.
¹¹The Lord gives strength to his people;
    the Lord blesses his people with peace.

The repetition of "Ascribe to the Lord" lends solemnity to the opening of the poem; there is no doubt we are listening in on something important here. The rumbling phrase, "the voice of the Lord," sounds like thunder; its cumulative effect is to prepare us to raise our own voices with those who cry "Glory!" in the poem's climax. Finally, between verses 9 and 10 there is a lull—the storm is over and God is pictured serenely enthroned "above it all." The resultant blessing is "peace."

Sometimes reading a different translation or paraphrase of the psalm will help listeners hear it afresh. Eugene Peterson grabs us with an unorthodox rendering of the opening lines of Psalm 29 (*The Message*):

> Bravo, God, bravo!
> Gods and all angels shout, "Encore!"
> In awe before the glory,
> in awe before God's visible power.
> Stand at attention!
> Dress your best to honor him!

Ask Probing Questions

My final suggestion for ways to explicate is to ask almost any question literary scholars ask of poems, not only in the study, but in the pulpit as well.[22] What is this psalm's setting in time (hour of the day, season of the year)? What is its physical setting (indoors or out, rural or urban)? Who is speaking in the poem? Who is the presumed reader? Is this stock metaphor of the psalmists used in its normal manner or is something unusual going on here?

Explication as the Whole of a Sermon

In addition to using explication for small sections of the sermon, an entire sermon might occasionally take the form of an explication. The whole sermon becomes a sustained curation of the literary aspects of the text and their contribution to the poem's message.[23] It will differ from a lecture in that other homiletical concerns are taken seriously; for example, in a classroom explication of a poem, application to listeners' lives will probably be ignored; in a sermon this should never happen. If the preacher handles the explication

---

22 For what to say about a poem, see Laurence Perrine, *Sound and Sense: An Introduction to Poetry, 6th ed.* (Harcourt, Brace, Jovanovich, 1982), 29. For help in literary analysis of psalms in particular, see Leland Ryken, *Words of Delight*, chapter 9.

23 See Abraham Kuruvilla, *A Manual for Preaching* (Baker Academic, 2019) on preaching as curation of Scriptural texts.

skillfully, application will be woven throughout, not tacked on in moralizing fashion at the end.

To demonstrate how a careful explication of a poem might work in the pulpit, look at the close reading of Psalm 84 in Appendix 2.

Strategy 7
Make Judicious Use of English Poetry

Why "judicious"? For one thing, a lot of people do not like poetry. They find it difficult, so they don't read it. But if the poetry of the Bible facilitates an encounter with God in ways that prose does not, shouldn't we who preach learn to appreciate the genre and help our listeners do so as well? And might we not hope that the poetry of our native tongue will work in concert with the poetry of the Hebrews to enrich our preaching of the psalms?

Preachers can, of course, use poetry in sermons on any genre, to illustrate a point or to flesh out the body of the sermon. But in a sermon on a poetic text, a poem might do more; it might very well echo the text itself, meaning not just *what* the preacher wants to say but meaning *in the way* the psalm means.

Creation psalms find an echo in Gerard Manley Hopkins's "Pied Beauty."

> Glory be to God for dappled things—
>   For skies of couple-colour as a brinded cow;
>   For rose-moles all in stipple upon trout that swim;
> Fresh-firecoal chestnut-falls; finches'
>   Landscape plotted and pieces— fold, fallow, and plough;
>   And all trades, their gear and tackle and trim.
> All things counter, original, spare, strange;
>   Whatever is fickle, freckled (who knows how?)
>   With swift, slow, sweet, sour, adazzle, dim;
> He fathers-forth whose beauty is past change:
>   Praise him.

Here is Hopkins again, this time with a poem that sounds like a lament psalm ("Thou art indeed just, Lord, if I contend"):

Thou art indeed just, Lord, if I contend
With thee; but, sir, so what I plead is just.
Why do sinners' ways prosper? And why must
Disappointment all I endeavor end?
Wert thou my enemy, O thou my friend,
How wouldst thou worse, I wonder, than thou dost
Defeat, thwart me?

Psalm 16:10 ("You will not abandon me to the grave.") faces death
with confidence. So does John Donne:

Death, be not proud, though some have called thee
Mighty and dreadful, for thou art not so;
For those whom thou think'st thou dost overthrow
Die not, poor Death, nor yet canst thou kill me.
(from Sonnet #10)

Other poems by Donne, like other poems in the Psalter, sound less
defiant in the face of death. This one recalls the plaintive cries of
psalmists who wonder if God has given them up for dead:

Thou hast made me, and shall thy work decay?
Repair me now, for now mine end doth haste,
I run to death, and death meets me as fast,
And all my pleasures are like yesterday;
I dare not move my dim eyes any way,
Despair behind, and death before doth cast
Such terror, and my feeble flesh doth waste
By sin in it, which it t'wards hell doth weigh;
Only thou art above, and when towards thee
By thy leave I can look, I rise again;
But our old subtle foe so tempteth me,
That not one hour myself I can sustain;
Thy Grace may wing me to prevent his art,
And thou like Adamant draw mine iron heart.

Maybe Donne had Psalm 88 in mind when writing this sonnet. Certainly the poem recalls some of the sentiments and phrasing of that bleak Psalm: "my life draws near the grave" (v. 3); "down to the pit" (v. 4); "my eyes are dim with grief" (v. 9).

Psalm 73:25–26 inspired the last of Charles Wesley's 6,500 hymns. The psalmist wrote:

> Whom have I in heaven but you?
>   And being with you, I desire nothing on earth.
> My flesh and heart may fail,
>   but God is the strength of my heart
>   and my portion forever.

From his deathbed Wesley wrote:

> In age and feebleness extreme,
> Who shall a helpless worm redeem?
> Jesus! my only hope thou art,
> Strength of my failing flesh and heart;
> O could I catch one smile from thee,
> And drop into eternity!

There's another reason for that qualifying word, "make *judicious* use of English poetry." Some poetry just will not work in the pulpit because it is too dense, too hard to grasp on one hearing. Many contemporary poems are extremely difficult to read. Ordinary syntax is scorned, new words are invented, verbs become nouns, nouns verbs. Even the trained reader with a copy of the poem in front of her may have to work hard to decode it. How will she fare hearing it read aloud in a sermon with no opportunity to decipher obscurities or discover interpretive clues from punctuation and layout? Trying to illuminate a biblical poem with a perplexing contemporary poem is about as effective as drawing on red paper with a red crayon.

The Psalms themselves were written to be readily grasped by the average worshipper. In fact, sophisticated literature lovers who approach the Hebrew Bible primarily for an aesthetic experience may be disappointed by how conventional its poetry is. But as Robert Alter reminds us:

> Such a reliance on the conventional is perfectly understandable. For a text that is to be chanted by pilgrims in procession on their way up to the Temple mount, or recited by a suppliant at the altar or by someone recovered from a grave illness offering a thanksgiving sacrifice, you do not want a lot of fancy footwork in the imagery and syntax; you want, in fact, an eloquent rehearsal of traditional materials and even traditional ways of ordering those materials in a certain sequence.[24]

Preachers will want to follow the psalmists' lead and steer clear of the arcane, the complex, and the overly metaphysical when we select poetry for the pulpit.

On the other hand, limericks, doggerel, Dr. Seuss and most cowboy poems will not do a lot for psalms sermons either. Their tone is too light. Suitable pulpit poetry will probably fall somewhere between T. S. Eliot and a Hallmark card. The obscure and the saccharine should both be avoided.

Accessible Pulpit Poetry

- *Chapters into Verse: Poetry in English Inspired by the Bible,* Volume I (Oxford University Press, 1993), contains hundreds of poems based on Old Testament texts (Volume II covers the New Testament).
- In *The Poet's Book of Psalms,* Laurence Wieder has collected renderings of all 150 canonical psalms by twenty-five poets from the sixteenth to the twentieth century (Harper, 1995).
- Other useful anthologies include *the Country of the Risen King,* (Baker, 1978), *The New Oxford Book of Christian Verse* (Oxford University Press, 1981), and *The Treasury of Religious Verse* (Revell, 1962).

---

24 *The Art of Biblical Poetry,* 112.

And let no preacher forget the hymn book! Many contemporary hymnals make the worship leader's job easier by indexing Scriptural allusions in the hymns. Better yet is Donald A. Spencer's *Hymn and Scripture Selection Guide* (Baker, 1993). This labor of love includes more than two thousand cross references of psalm texts with the hymns and songs of the church.

A glance at one of these indices reveals how many praise songs and hymn texts spring from the Psalter:

"How Majestic is Thy Name"	Psalm 8
"The Spacious Firmament on High"	Psalm 19
"The King of Love My Shepherd is"	Psalm 23
"Unto Thee O Lord"	Psalm 25
"As the Deer"	Psalm 42
"Clap Your Hands, All Ye Nations"	Psalm 47
"O God our Help in Ages Past"	Psalm 90
"Praise, My Soul, the King of Heaven"	Psalm 103

These are just a few representative hymns. Hundreds of others pick up themes and phrases from the psalms. The preacher who quotes them may find that their familiarity reinforces the impact of the sermon, especially if worshippers hum or sing them all week long.

The preacher might use a metrical version of the psalm itself.[25] Or read a contemporary version of it.[26] A sermon on Psalm 56 could conclude with Eugene Peterson's paraphrase:

> God, you did everything you promised,
>   and I'm thanking you with all my heart.
> You pulled me from the brink of death,
>   my feet from the cliff-edge of doom.

---

25 There are many collections available, including *The Book of Psalms for Singing* (Reformed Presbyterian Church of North America, 1973); *The Psalms of David in Metre* (Presbyterian Heritage, 1991); Coverdale's melodious version in *The Book of Common Prayer*. Many hymnals include a selection of metrical Psalms.

26 Creative renderings include Leslie Brandt, *Psalms Now* 3rd ed. (Concordia, 2004); Richard S. Hanson, *The Psalms in Modern Speech* (Fortress, 1968); not to mention hundreds of well-done musical versions of all styles.

Now I stroll at leisure with God
in the sunlit fields of life.

Three Points and a Poem?

When preachers meet for coffee, chances are somebody will crack
a joke about sermons consisting of "three points and a poem." We
all know how overworked that classic pattern can be. But maybe
there is more to its popularity than lazy over-reliance on it. There *is*
something aesthetically satisfying about *three*. And there is something that feels, well, right about concluding a sermon with a hymn
or poem. Henry Mitchell, who argues that sermons should ordinarily build toward celebration, says that the end of the sermon
calls for heightened style and poetic language.[27] Any strategy can
be overworked. But we should not be embarrassed or surprised if,
after immersing ourselves in the meaning and mood of poetic texts
(and not just through force of habit) we find ourselves drawn to
poetry when concluding our sermons on the psalms.

For Further Study

Alter, Robert. *The Art of Biblical Poetry.* Basic Books, 1985.
Petersen, David L. and Kent Harold Richards, *Interpreting Hebrew
   Poetry.* Fortress, 1992.
Ryken, Leland. *Words of Delight.* Baker, 1992.
Wieder, Laurence. *The Poets' Book of Psalms.* Harper Collins, 1995.

Talk about It

- Discuss the pros and cons of explication as a homiletical strategy. How effective do you think the explication of Psalm 84 in
  Appendix 2 is *as a sermon*?
- Look at the psalms that employ refrain (page 59). Choose one
  (other than those discussed in this chapter), and describe what
  use a preacher might make of that refrain in a sermon.

---

27 Henry Mitchell, *Celebration and Experience in Preaching* (Abingdon,
1990), 68–69.

Dig Deeper

Identify three psalms with a chiastic structure. For at least one of these, decide what use a preacher might make of this poetic device in structuring a sermon on the psalm.

Practice

Write an outline for a sermon on Psalm 119 that tries to preserve the rhetorical effect of its acrostic design.

5

Words

If . . . words are to enter men's hearts and bear fruit, they must be the right words shaped cunningly to pass men's defenses and explode silently and effectually within their minds.[1]
J. B. Phillips

Like apples of gold in settings of silver is a word fitly spoken.
Proverbs 25:11

Mark Twain was right: "The difference between the right word and the nearly right word is the difference between lightning and the lightning bug."[2] We preachers are ever in search of the right word: the noun that paints a thousand pictures, the verb that ratchets understanding forward several notches. We're dissatisfied with the nearly right words we hear ourselves uttering week in and week out. We're haunted by the provocative turn of phrase in someone else's sermon and wonder, "How did he come up with that?" Our quest is that of Qoheleth, who "searched to find just the right words" (Ecclesiastes 12:10).

We're after lightning, not lightning bugs.

---

1 Cited by Sue Nichols, *Words on Target* (John Knox Press, 1963), 50.

2 Caroline Thomas Harnsberger, *Everyone's Mark Twain* (A.S. Barnes and Company, 1972), 669.

Strategy 8
Pay Attention to Words

Good word choice will improve any sermon, but especially sermons on psalms. Poets use words differently, and sermons on poems should respect this difference – not only in exegesis when we discover the meaning in authors' words, but in delivery when we use our own words to facilitate fresh experiences of texts. So what marks the right words, the "words fitly spoken" which will help carry the poetic message of our Psalm texts?

Compression

Poetic language is compressed, densely packed. A word is heavy, a phrase weighs a ton. At the heart of any definition of poetry is insight compressed into brevity. Poetry is "a kind of language that says more and says it more intensely than does ordinary language."[3] In poetry we discover, in Marlowe's words, "infinite riches in a little room."

Where prose may take a page and a half to argue that justice should be tempered with mercy, and moral rectitude balanced with compassion for those who fall short, poetry says, "Righteousness and peace kiss each other" (Ps 85:10). Where a commentary or sermon might use exposition, examples and quotations to depict the deathly effects of ungodly speech, poetry says, "Their throat is an open grave" (Ps 5:9). In poetry, less is more.

Which is not to say that poetry is always briefer than prose. The psalmist could have written, "My heart is heavy," but he (well, the translator, anyway) used twice as many words to say, "My heart is blighted and withered like grass" (102:4). What matters is not word count but that every word count.

If poetry accomplishes its work with tight-packed words, perhaps our sermons on poetry should attempt the same. One way to respect the poemness of our text is to use compressed language, as Elizabeth Achtemeier does when preaching Psalm 148. Painting a

---

3 Laurence Perrine, *Sound and Sense: An Introduction to Poetry*, 6th ed. (Harcourt, Brace, Jovanovich, 1973), 2.

picture of a God exuberant over all he has made, she says more in four words than some people say in four paragraphs: "The Creator loves pizzazz!"[4] The sentence is perfect. It not only says a lot with a little, it does a lot with a little. "Pizzazz" puts a smile on our faces, surely one of the intended effects of Psalm 148.

If we want sermons to work like the psalm texts on which they are based, we'll make words count. We'll craft economical sentences where not a syllable can be dropped without loss. We'll prune away verbal dead wood: lengthy citation of sources, irrelevant explanations, pointless words like "very" and "really." Listeners will have to hang on every word, just like they do when they are hearing a poem, lest they miss something.

One relatively easy way to compress language in sermons on psalms is to avoid the kind of connective words we might ordinarily use in more discursive sermon styles: "secondly," "another reason," "consequently," and so forth. Such marks of logical order are better suited to a discursive speaking style than to the poetic feel that a genre-sensitive preacher will want to give a sermon on a poem. Certainly a sermon on a psalm has to be coherent: listeners need to sense connections and progress toward a goal. But other, more poetic stylistic devices can give the sermon its sense of order: parallel phrasing, refrain, returning to the sermon's central image, repetition of a key word, rhythm in speech, physical movement – any of these might serve to tie the sermon together and mark its progress without sacrificing the tightness, the compression of poetic speech.

If a preacher says, "This psalm gives us another and even more fundamental reason for trusting God when our lives are threatened; let's look at verse 5," the structure is logical. If the preacher describes a threatening experience and then says, "But God is a refuge [pause] read it [pause] God is a refuge [pause] solid [pause] strong [pause] a mighty tower, a refuge," and trusts the listener to make the connection for herself, then the structure is poetic. If the preacher says, "This psalm includes both sadness and happiness," the style is prosaic. If he says, "Deep shadow and flashes of sunlight

---

4 The sermon, "God, the Nature Lover," is in *Nature, God and Pulpit* (Eerdmans, 1992), 40–49. Achtemeier is quoting Annie Dillard.

play throughout the stanzas of this poem," the style is poetic.

Specificity

Poets do not simply "look" at things. They glare, gaze, scrutinize, survey, contemplate, ogle, peer, or peep, and we find ourselves doing the same through their eyes. They do not say that "So and so *went*." They say that she ambled, sped, tore, skipped, looped, loped, scampered, or whirled. "She went" only tells me that she got from point A to point B. "She slithered" conveys a whole lot more: something of the subject's character and the revulsion I feel in the presence of literal snakes. All with one word.

Listen to David Thompson on Psalm 150:6:

> *"Let everything that has breath praise the LORD!"*
> All breath? All breath! Everything that breathes? Everything!
> That is, praise the Lord with the wag of the puppy dog's tail.
> Praise God with the arch of the golden eagle's sail. Praise the
> Lord with the leap of leopard and lynx. The ox, the ass, the
> elephant and its trunk; the fox, the bass, the elegant and the
> skunk. With fur, with fin, with beak, with bill; with claw, with
> paw, with quack, with quill, with wing, with web, with tail,
> without, the last line of the Psalm shouts out, *"Let everything
> that has breath praise the LORD!"*[5]

This sermon conclusion works well partly because of assonance, consonance, and rhyme, but mostly because the preacher makes the word "everything" more specific.

Specificity often has to do with connotation. Consider these pairs of words: chest/breast, red/crimson, book/tome, trousers/britches, scholar/egghead, zealot/fanatic. However similar their dictionary definitions may be, the two words in each pair are *not* identical. They evoke different images and emotions. So do the words "preacher," "minister," "cleric," "reverend," "pastor," "parson," and "shepherd." The same person may be referred to by any

---

5 David L. Thompson, "Praise the Lord!" *Pulpit Digest* (July/August 1992): 51–53.

of these labels, but each has its own connotations, its own emotional tone. Preachers will want to pay attention to connotations in choosing their words.

Although the average American's day-to-day vocabulary runs to a few thousand words, English has more than half a million. Maybe with help from a thesaurus or dictionary of synonyms, the preacher can find the right words, specific words, "lightning" words to speak the poetic Word of God.

If time-consuming attention to vocabulary seems impractical on a weekly basis, maybe the preacher can at least work on word choice when preaching psalms. We can reread our manuscripts before Sunday morning, scrap all the lazy, generic words and substitute their more exact cousins. But not just exact; let's aim for energetic, colorful, living words. The right words are *vital* words.

Vitality

A speaker serves up this ho-hum line as the third main point in a prosaic message on Psalm 46: "God is at work in the world to achieve peace." Well (yawn) okay. If I'm still awake after points one and two I may have to agree that this is a truth worth knowing. But where, oh where is the vitality of the text: "He makes wars cease to the ends of the earth; he breaks the bow and shatters the spear, he burns the shields with fire" (46:9)? If the sermon has to state a third "point," why not let that vibrant sentence be it?

At a seminary commencement, the congregation is urged to emulate the righteous king of Psalm 72. The preacher tells graduates that "a godly leader will be a blessing to his people." Well, maybe so, but after listening to ten minutes of banalities you do not feel like being a blessing to anybody; you just want this ceremony to end. It's being held outside, it's hot, your head droops. Your eye falls on the speaker's text, printed in the program, and though you would not know it from his speech, it is a vivid, vital text. The king (or, broadened for applicability to this audience, the godly leader) ". . . will be like rain falling on a mown field, like showers watering the earth" (72:6). As the speaker drones on, the psalmist's words give you an idea. You circulate a note to your fellow-sufferers in the stands: "Pray for rain!"

Sue Nichols says, "The Bible calls the messages of God goads that try the soul; sword-blades that pierce to the division of soul and spirit, joints and marrow. So often we make them meringue."[6] She's right. And she models the livelier communication for which she's pleading: "meringue" strikes me as the perfect word. Would I have thought of it if I were writing on the subject? Probably not. Does that mean that all I can do is envy the wizards who conjure up such words? No. I can work hard at word choice so as to improve my customary performance.

"To Be?" No, Not "To Be"

For greater vitality, we'll minimize use of the verb "to be." "Is," "was," "are," and "were" yield sentences as mushy as yesterday's corn flakes. Active verbs snap, crackle, and pop.

Not	But
Lord, your creation is bountiful.	You crown the year with your bounty, and your carts overflow with abundance (Psalm 65:11).
We were in grave danger of being destroyed.	The floods would have engulfed us, the torrent would have swept over us (124:4).
Such a conclusion to the psalms is surprising.	Now such an end to the psalms surprises us (David Thompson on Psalm 150).

Where it seems an active verb does not fit and "to be" is the only choice, try one of these:

animates	embraces	instills	shapes
appears	enfolds	involves	stays
arises	enhances	looms	substitutes

---

6 Nichols, *Words on Target*, 47.

composes	enlivens	promotes	succeeds
constitutes	establishes	pulses	supports
creates	formulates	remains	undergirds
develops	generates	replaces	shapes

"To be" is not to be avoided altogether. It may be just right when combined with other, stronger verbs, or with striking statements or questions: "Why did God make the world? It is a question that philosophers and theologians have wrestled with for centuries: Why is there something? Why not nothing?"[7] Or when we want to make a comparison: "His whole life was a sob. It is only those who know what it is to be haunted who know what it is to be happy."[8] Or when we want to slow the sermon down to a contemplative pace: "The Lord is my Shepherd."

Generally, though, if vitality is our aim, we'll recast sluggish "to be" sentences with spirited verbs.[9]

Sense Appeal

Sermons on psalms should appeal to our senses. Psalms themselves certainly do so. They do not settle for "I'm sad," but say "My strength is dried up like a potsherd, and my tongue sticks to the roof of my mouth" (Ps 22:15). The psalmists do not desire God in some ethereal, other-worldly fashion; they crave God with physical, tangible desire. Psalm 63, for instance, speaks of thirst, longing, lips, hunger; and (a tactile image) "on my bed I remember you." No sermon on this text can do it justice by reducing it to bloodless abstractions.

---

7 Elizabeth Achtemeier, "God the Music Lover," on Psalm 148

8 Frank Boreham, "Scepter and Song," on Psalm 51:3

9 This chapter's preference for active verbs and the active voice has to do with vivid *English* style; it makes no claim to reflect *Hebrew* poetics. The systems of poetry have much in common (notably, affective, imaginative, and aesthetic concerns), but how they use words and sentences to accomplish their poetic aims differs significantly.

Spurgeon knew something about sense appeal when preaching the psalms.[10] He engaged imaginations by appealing to:

Sight. "Never cease your prayers. No time is ill for prayer. The glare of daylight should not tempt you to cease; and the gloom of midnight should not make you stop your cries" ("Unanswered Prayer," on Psalm 22:2).[11] Note not only the sense appeal but the nicely alliterated antithesis between "glare" and "gloom."

Hearing. Preaching on the "new song" of Psalm 40:3, Spurgeon spoke of praising, weeping, sighing, chanting, moaning, groaning, roaring, thundering, crying, talking, spitting, squeaking, and singing (of course we'd expect him to say "singing," but forty times?). He spoke of hymns, vespers, a thousand tongues, sweet voices, cant, merriment, operas, and lyrics; discord and doggerel, nightingale and noise; hosannas and hallelujahs, verses and choruses, musical scores, the deep base of confession and the high notes of "jubilates" that rise even to the skies ("The New Song on Earth," on Psalm 40).

Taste, Touch, and Smell. Speaking of the power of God's Word, Spurgeon says that the gospel itself, not its imperfect herald, is what matters, "however roughly the meat may be carved, and however it may be served up on the coarsest platter." Later he says that God's pity-tempered discipline makes his children "smart, and cry, and groan, and sigh," but "there is not one twig too many in the rod, nor one stroke over the right number, not one drop of gall too much, and that is none too bitter." Elsewhere, "Never once has the clay fallen on the coffin lid . . . without the pity of your God falling on your heart, like gentle dew from heaven" ("Our Heavenly Father's Pity," on Psalm 103:13).

---

10 And not only the psalms. Scarcely a paragraph in Spurgeon's published sermons fails to engage sight, hearing, taste, touch, or smell. Jay Adams wrote a master's thesis on word choice in the great preacher's work and published it as *Sense Appeal in the Sermons of Charles Haddon Spurgeon; Studies in Preaching, Volume 1* (Presbyterian and Reformed, 1976).

11 This and the following excerpts are from the *Library of Spurgeon's Sermons,* Charles T. Cook, ed., volume 9, *C.H. Spurgeon's Sermons on the Psalms* (Zondervan, 1960).

Granted, some of Spurgeon's sentences sound quaint now. We will not talk exactly like he did. But we can take a tip from the Prince of Preachers and pepper our speaking with sense appeal. "Words come in textures; words are hard or smooth or squishy soft. Words have colors; they are pastel, they are bold. They are neutral. They are colorless. . . . Words are sharp, words are blunt; words have edges that are keen. There are scalpel words and razor words and words that have a saber's slash. Words are dull, words are sparkling. Words are alive, they are languid. Words fly, sail, drive, race, creep, crawl. So many words! If we are patient – if we will work at the task – we will begin to find the right ones."[12]

For Further Study

Preachers interested in exploring how poetic devices can find a place in oral speech will find helpful advice in:

Arnold, Carroll C. *Criticism of Oral Rhetoric.* Charles E. Merrill, 1974. Pages 126–138.
Campbell, Karlyn Kohrs. *The Rhetorical Act.* Wadsworth Publishing Company, 1982. Pages 210–212.
Larson, Craig Brian. "Seven Habits of Highly Effective Preachers." *Leadership* 15 (Summer 1994): 88–93.

David Powlison invites those who communicate God's Word publicly and privately (in counseling) to learn how to use words from the psalmists: http://www.ccef.org/blog/those-who-words.

Talk about It

Describe a recent example of striking word choice. Maybe you heard it in a sermon, a speech, or even in a classroom lecture or conversation. Whatever the incident, the speaker chose just the right word or words to say what needed to be said. If you and your conversation partners cannot think of any examples, what does that tell you?

---

12 James J. Kilpatrick, *Fine Print* (Andrews and McMeel, 1993), 8.

Dig Deeper

For improving word choice, check out Sue Nichols, *Words on Target* (Westminster John Knox, 1976), or William Zinsser, *On Writing Well* (HarperCollins, 1990).

Practice

Reread your notes for a sermon you've preached (or a published sermon). See if you can improve specificity and vitality by changing ten words.

6

Orality

T.S. Eliot is supposed to have said that it is the purpose of literature to turn blood into ink. If that is true, and I believe it is, and if it is further true that sermons may be thought of as a specific type of literature, whether they are actually written out in full or not, then it is the purpose of speaking that sermonic literature to turn the ink back into blood.
Charles Bartow[1]

Strategy 9
Practice an Oral Delivery that
Helps Carry the Poet's Meaning

"Boring? *My* sermon boring? You've got to be kidding!" I thought my professor had listened to the wrong student's tape by mistake. I'd submitted two sample messages for critique as part of a D.Min. seminar. One, of which I was particularly proud, was on Psalm 127 ("Unless the Lord builds the house. . ."). Astute, humorous, well-illustrated and practical; I thought it was a model sermon.

And I also felt passionately about it. My wife and I have seven children, and over the years we've noticed occasional stares at the mall or heard condescending comments from people who find our "full quiver" unseemly. My sermon championed the psalmist's

---

1 Quoted in Robin R. Meyers, *With Ears to Hear: Preaching as Self-Persuasion* (The Pilgrim Press, 1993), 117.

claim, "Sons are a heritage from the Lord, children are a reward from him," as one who knows from experience what the poet is talking about.

So I was stunned when my teacher said the sermon did not hold his attention. He said that he'd listened to the tape while driving and had to work hard to stay focused. At first I thought the problem was his. Maybe he had other things on his mind. Maybe he was prejudiced against large families and didn't like what I said in my message. Maybe his tape player needed batteries.

But then I listened to the tape myself and had to agree that it was, well, boring. My delivery was flat. The passion I felt for my subject did not come through. The humorous anecdotes about family life elicited little more than an occasional chuckle. A potentially good sermon was spoiled by a ho-hum delivery.

My instructor's prescribed remedy? Nothing all that earth-shaking—just practice. Out loud. Practice delivering sermons before delivering them. Preferably more than once.

Practicing a sermon strikes some of us as artificial. In one of my favorite *Leadership* cartoons, a preacher poses before a full length mirror, one hand gripping his Bible, the other pointing a bony finger toward hell, eyes bulging, mouth skewed in perverse pleasure as he rehearses the one word, "Baaahrrrrimmmmmstone-uh!"

The cartoon effectively caricatures those in the ministerial guild who strive to project a special pulpit persona. But that's not the goal of sanctified preparation. Practice can free the biblical message to be heard more effectively, and is in itself no more artificial than is writing a sermon manuscript. Practice reminds us that preaching is *performance* in the non-pejorative sense of that term, "form coming through." The goal of practice is congruity between the written text and the oral event of the sermon.

Before receiving that blunt criticism from my homiletics prof, I used to spend Sunday morning writing out my sermon word for word. Though I did not carry this manuscript into the pulpit, the final re-write gave me one last chance to fine-tune word choice and screw the sermon into my memory. Now I try to finish this stage of preparation earlier in the week or even skip it if necessary to make sure I have time for oral rehearsal on Sunday morning. The result is a livelier delivery, one in which the text and what people hear are more in sync. This approach is especially apt when preaching the psalms because so much of poetry's meaning depends on how it sounds.

Noisemakers and Kneelers

"Noisemakers and Kneelers" is a fitting title for Robert Hubbard's sermon on Psalm 95. It captures both the division of the poem between verses five and six, and the vocal variety with which Hubbard delivers the sermon. The psalm's first stanza calls to worshippers, "Come, let us sing for joy to the Lord; let us shout aloud to the Rock of our salvation." It applauds Yahweh as "the great God, the great King above all gods," whose hands formed and possess all creation from Everest's icy summit to ocean depths where blind fish swim. Hubbard preaches these lines with energy. He's expansive and celebratory.

The hymn's second stanza also begins with "Come," but now with a different tone. This time we are urged to come as repentant kneelers who will not to imitate our fathers' hardheartedness and rebellion. Appropriately, Hubbard's delivery slows down and gets quieter. He sounds more pastoral as he appeals to the sheep of God's pasture. His softer volume shares the burden of communicating the second stanza's mood.

Intensification

Effective delivery often works in the opposite direction, building in intensity as the sermon progresses. E. V. Hill, preaching "Three Fatal Mistakes" on Psalm 1:1–2, punctuated his sermon with the key word "fatal" to warn the congregation away from "the way of sinners." Spoken almost matter-of-factly at first, the word became a spray of gunfire by sermon's end: "fatal, fatal, fatal, fatal, FATAL!" Hill had by that point demonstrated how deadly it is to ignore God's law. Poignant examples gleaned from many years of pastoral experience had prepared his hearers for this final crescendo of warning, "Fatal."

Sometimes the text calls for intensification as unmistakably as if the poet had scrawled *fortissimo* in the margin. Psalm 13, for example, cries "How long?" four times in four lines. "How long? How long? How long? How long?" It is hard to imagine preaching this lament without increasing the pathos of each successive plea.

Pace, Pitch, Punch, Pause, and More

Intensity is not the only vocal variable that can be enhanced by re-hearsing sermons aloud. Phrasing, pitch, articulation, pace (along with blocking) all help carry the meaning of the text and can be improved with practice.

Am I preaching Psalm 88, the bleakest of the laments? My voice had better sound sad. Psalm 79, a complaint? The congregation should hear in my voice genuine grief over the state of God's cause in the world and something like—what, pique? frustration? impatience?—that God seems so slow to remedy the situation. If I am preaching Psalm 148, my words should spill out as if twenty minutes is too little time to summon all creation to the worship of God. There's a difference, however, between a fast pace that says, "I'm breathless because there's so much to tell," and one that says, "This is trivial, we can dispense with it quickly."

A voice coach, a public speaking text, a D. Min. seminar, or an online sermon evaluation service could help a preacher analyze where help on vocal variety is needed and suggest some practice exercises. The operative word is "practice." We cannot make delivery match content by reading the manuscript silently and scribbling marginal notes like "raise pitch here," "speak slowly," or "downward inflection." We have to *taste* the words. We have to savor the meanings they bear when spoken aloud, and the meanings of our silences as well. After preaching we will want to listen to a recording, decide what worked well and what did not, and decide how to improve our next practice and performance.[2]

---

2 Al Fasol's *A Guide to Self-Improvement in Sermon Delivery* (Baker, 1983) promotes simultaneous use of a manuscript and a tape for refining delivery (pp. 58–72 and Appendix C). Carl Hoefler's thoughts on writing an oral manuscript are also helpful: *Creative Preaching and Oral Writing* (C.S.S. Publishing, 1978)

A related strategy is to practice good oral interpretation of the text itself.

Strategy 10
Read the Psalm Well

Years ago, I was the guest preacher for a Lenten series at another church in town. I arrived half an hour before the service for a sound check, and discovered I was not the only early bird. A teenager, the lay reader for evening, stood at the microphone rehearsing the Scripture text. His pastor listened from various locations in the sanctuary, coaching him on projection, pronunciation, and phrasing. I was impressed by how seriously they took the Scripture reading, and felt guilty for times I had handed someone a text five minutes before the service started and asked her to wing it.

Respect for God's Word requires that we read it well. This starts in the study. Ronald Allen, who includes several oral readings of his text as part of sermon preparation, reminds us:

> Much of the Bible has a long oral history. Before it was put into written form, and even after, much of the Bible was intended for the ear and the mouth (to be heard, spoken, or sung) rather than for the eye (to be read). Reading aloud, therefore, may set in motion intuitive sympathy with the text. If done with expression, consonant with the tone of the text, it may call to consciousness some of the feelings that would have been evoked by the text in its original setting.[3]

So the preacher, alone at first, opens up the psalm's possibilities by reading it aloud. Then it's the congregation's turn to hear it. Before a word of the sermon is spoken, they experience the text through oral interpretation, "the act of communicating to an audience a work of literary art in its intellectual, emotional, and aesthetic

---

though his suggestion that preachers write, record, rewrite, record, and listen to a sermon four times before public delivery is unrealistic.

3 Ronald Allen, *Contemporary Biblical Interpretation for Preachers* (Judson, 1984), 25.

entirety."[4] Before the pastor begins a sermon on Psalm 1, the congregation has already begun to sense from the reading of the poem something of the difference between the righteous and the wicked. Every line describing the godly person was drawn out, spoken unhurriedly, allowing listeners time to imagine deep roots, life-giving streams, and the fruit of a Torah-oriented life. The reading of verses 1–3 sounded pastoral, reflective, almost ponderous. Then, "Not so the wicked. They are like the chaff that the wind blows away." The lines were spoken and done with almost before the listener realized it, delivered with a barely perceptible shrug of the reader's shoulder that signaled that there is not a whole lot to be said about the wicked. They're chaff. Not much to them.

Before a sermon on Psalm 12, liturgists have performed the poem, letting the congregation hear the different "voices" in this dramatic dialogue.[5] Before a sermon on Psalm 13, the congregation has already begun to sense the poignancy of the poem through a sensitive reading of "How long?" Before a sermon on Psalm 29, the congregation has already experienced its two moods, awe-inspiring storm and serenity, because two readers skillfully interpreted the text that morning. One rendered the thundering voice of God, another with a softer voice introduced the text and then wrapped up the reading with a gentler rendition of verses 10 and 11, "The Lord blesses his people with peace."

Successful interpretation of the text is so vital for the congregation's grasp of its message that preachers should, perhaps, read it

---

4 Lee and Gura, *Oral Interpretation,* 8th ed. (Houghton Mifflin, 1992), 3. Jack Rang urges us not to emphasize the intellectual so much that we forget other dimensions of the text. "Our task is not merely to bring a message to an audience but to bring an *experience* which can be shared. More often it is our responsibility to set a mood or bring about an indirect response from the audience. And that sort of response is often centered more on listeners' emotions than on their intellect." *How to Read the Bible Aloud* (Paulist, 1994), 3.

5 Carl J. Bosma discusses the voices in the Psalms and implications for liturgists and preachers in view of the performative nature of language. "Discerning the Voices in the Psalms: A Discussion of Two Problems in Psalmic Interpretation, Part 2," *Calvin Theological Journal* 44 (2009): 127–170. Psalm 12 is discussed on pages 136–143.

themselves, if at all possible.[6] This may be particularly good advice for psalm texts, since poetry can be made unintelligible by a poor reading or performed so well that we wonder if a sermon is necessary. Of course, if others in the congregation are gifted readers, then by all means they should be used for this important work. But preachers, even seasoned preachers, can and should grow in their ability to communicate texts by skillful reading.

Several years ago I visited a church whose long-tenured pastor obviously loved preaching and loved his people. Unfortunately, his warm, personable, note-free sermon delivery did not carry over to his reading of Scripture. When, in the middle of the sermon, it was time to read the text, he fumbled for his place on the page. He read without expression. His Bible rested on a pulpit which was too low for him, so his reading seemed addressed to the floor. When he finished reading and resumed preaching, we saw his face again. His voice came alive again. The unintended message about the Bible reading was, "Well, that's over; now for the important stuff."

Oral Reading Do's and Do Nots

A thorough treatment of oral interpretation is outside the scope of this book. Those interested in more on the subject could check out *Devote Yourself to the Public Reading of Scripture* by Jeffrey Arthurs, *How to Read the Bible Aloud* by Jack Rang, or *Reading Scripture in Public* by Thomas McComiskey.[7] Arthurs's book includes a DVD; Rang and McComiskey devote chapters to reading biblical

---

6 Ian Pitt-Watson, *A Primer for Preachers* (Baker, 1986), 89–90. Some churches are blessed with competent readers, and pastors would be foolish to overlook them. We ought to develop teams of skilled lectors, oral interpreters, and reader's theater groups. See Gordon C. Bennett, *Reader's Theater Comes to Church* (Meriwether, 1985); and Jeffrey D. Arthurs, *Devote Yourself to the Public Reading of Scripture* (Kregel, 2012), 117–128.

7 Jeffrey D. Arthurs, *Devote Yourself to the Public Reading of Scripture* (Kregel, 2012); Jack Rang, *How to Read the Bible Aloud*; Thomas McComiskey, *Reading Scripture in Public* (Baker, 1991); Charles Bartow, *Effective Speech Communication in Leading Worship* (Abingdon, 1988); Robert Jacks, *Getting the Word Across: Speech Communication for Pastors and Lay Leaders* (Eerdmans, 1995).

poetry. Here, distilled from these and other sources, are a few suggestions for reading psalms aloud.

Do not read the text in public without first practicing it in private. *Do* rehearse the oral reading over several sessions. A few brief rehearsals are better than one long one. For a doctoral seminar on pulpit delivery I practiced my text thirty times before performing it. That kind of time investment is not practical for every sermon, but with experience, it's not necessary either.

Do not jump prematurely into oral rehearsal. *Do* make sure you understand the psalm before trying to convey that understanding vocally. Exegesis precedes technique. What's the mood of this petition in Psalm 27:7?

> Hear my voice when I call, O Lord;
>   be merciful to me and answer me.

Is the psalmist angry? Or quietly confident of receiving the answer he desires? Try reading these lines with fists clenched, lips tight. Now read them again with head bowed, hands open and just the hint of a smile. Hear the difference? In this case, context rules out an angry tone, and you would not want to have practiced that misreading. Experimenting with different sounds can help you get at meaning, but repeated rehearsal before you are sure of the meaning is a bad idea.

Do exaggerate during rehearsal. This will impress interpretive options on your mind and lower inhibitions, giving you more freedom when it comes time for the public reading. *Do not* exaggerate in front of the congregation. A young man in one of my former parishes impressed me one morning with an energetic Scripture reading. So I asked him to read a few more times. After several Sundays, it became clear that his volume and pace knobs were stuck on "loud" and "gallop." Psalms, proverbs, narratives, and epistles all sounded the same: exaggerated, with no regard for the content or mood of the text. Sometimes the results were comical.

Do not make large gestures. Oral interpretation is not acting but is a more subtle performance relying on voice, facial expression, and barely perceptible adjustments of upper body and posture. *Do* hold your head and Bible up so people can hear your voice and read your face.

Do make eye contact. If you're well prepared, an occasional glance at the text may be sufficient. Most of the time your eyes will be on the congregation. But *do not* play peek-a-boo with the congregation over the top of your Bible. It would be better to keep your eyes glued to the page for the entire reading than to force a head-bobbing, staccato eye contact.

If the psalm is a prayer, consider forgoing eye contact altogether: address the reading to God and let the congregation listen in. I once preached an entire sermon on Ephesians 1:15–23 in prayer form. I sat on a stool, looked toward heaven, and prayed for my people using Paul's words and my own. In retrospect, twenty minutes was too long to go without eye contact. But for the time it takes to read a psalm, people can watch you speak the words of the text back to God.

Do not botch pronunciation. I heard a layman who had been asked to read a tongue-tying list of biblical names gamely finish his text and then add, "That's hard to say when you're wearing false teeth!" I laughed sympathetically along with everyone else. But I cannot cut myself the same slack. It's one thing to make a volunteer feel okay about stumbling over hard words; it's another to excuse sloppy reading by a professional minister. I display disrespect for my text if I butcher it.

Names, of course, are not the only traps for readers. In several translations, Psalm 18:9 reads, "He bowed the heavens and came down." Is this *bō,* to bend into a curve, or *bau,* to incline the head or body? Clearly, it must be the first, and the liturgist should figure this out before reading the passage publicly.

Do convey the psalm's parallelism by pausing slightly between the parts of each line. *Do not,* however, get stuck in a sing-song delivery by making every pause equal.

Consider Psalm 18:7:

The earth trembled and quaked,
and the foundations of the mountains shook;
they trembled because he was angry.

If you read this verse with no pause after "quaked," it will sound like prose. But if you hesitate briefly at the comma, you will fix in listeners' minds the first five words as one of three parallel portions in the poetic line. A longer pause is called for after "shook," as indicated by the semicolon. In the next verse we find the longer pause coming first:

> Smoke rose from his nostrils;
>> consuming fire came from his mouth,
>> burning coals blazed out of it.

The last two cola are bound together by the shared image of God's mouth, so the pause between them is briefer than the one separating both from the first. Paying attention to punctuation can help us distinguish each colon without making all of them the same in length and stress.

Parallel words should ordinarily receive parallel stress: "quaked," "shook," and the second "trembled" in verse 7 should be read with approximately the same force, although "trembled" could bear a bit more since it climaxes the series and prepares us for the summary word, "angry."

Similarly, in verse 8, we want to give equal weight to "smoke," "consuming fire" and "burning coals." "Nostrils" and "mouth" will get parallel stress, a little softer than the three key terms. Of course, it would sound absurd to stress the final word, "it" as strongly as its parallels in the preceding cola.

Some oral interpreters find it helpful to type or photocopy their selection. Bold print, italics, caps, underlines and highlighter pen can cue variations and similarities in delivery. Slant marks may indicate stops, the more slant marks, the longer the stop.

> *The earth* trembled and quaked, /
> and *the foundations of the mountains* shook; //
> they trembled because he was angry. ///
> Smoke rose from his *nostrils*; //
> consuming fire came from his *mouth*, /
> burning coals blazed out of it.

Verse 9 and 10 read:

> He parted the heavens and came down;
>> dark clouds were under his feet.
> He mounted on the cherubim and flew;
>> he soared on the wings of the wind.

Our rendering of the key words "down" and "soared" will make or break the oral interpretation of these two lines. "Down" must have a note of finality, even though it comes mid-sentence. We can give it a heavy sound by drawing it out, inflecting downward, and pausing as long as we do for any of the full stops. We will read verse 9 faster than the preceding lines, our voice soaring on "soared," but without overacting, and then finish by drawing out the final words almost as if they were one, "wings-of-the-wind," savoring the initial consonants in "wings" and "wind."

Verses 11–15 should be read with building intensity, louder and faster, as God's earth-rending storm breaks.

> He made the darkness his covering, his canopy around him –
>> the dark rain clouds of the sky.
> Out of the brightness of his presence clouds advanced,
>> with hailstones and bolts of lightning.
> The voice of the Lord thundered from heaven;
>> the voice of the Most High resounded.
> He shot his arrows and scattered the enemies.
>> great bolts of lightning and routed them.
> The valleys of the sea were exposed
>> and the foundations of the earth were laid bare
> at your rebuke, O Lord, at the blast of breath from your nostrils.

Then, a decided rest before verse 16:

> He reached down from on high and took hold of me;
>> he drew me out of deep waters.

Before speaking these words, the reading comes to a full stop for several seconds. We let the echoes of God's nostril blast die away. We change the direction of our gaze: while addressing God directly in verse 15, we looked at the "God spot" on the balcony wall; now we let our eyes slowly meet the congregation's, still not saying a word. Then, just the hint of a smile and a subtle relaxing of the shoulders signal a mood change. We look at the Bible, prolonging the silence. Then, eyes back on the congregation, no doubt about the smile now, "He reached down from on high and took hold of me."

If this kind of detailed attention to reading the text seems a bit much for the busy pastor, we might ask ourselves how highly we regard the words of Scripture? I will never forget the rebuke of a theologically liberal preacher to his more conservative cousin: "You evangelicals devote all your energy to the sermon and none to the reading of the text. You claim to hold a high view of inspiration, but you're more interested in what the preacher has to say about the Bible than what the Bible itself says." Ouch!

Paul urges us to "Give attention to the public reading of Scripture" (1 Tim 4:13). We might measure our obedience to this exhortation by asking:

- Did I read at a pace that allowed hearers to grasp the message of the text?
- Did I stumble during the reading or mispronounce words?
- Did I emphasize what was most important in the passage?
- Did I use pause effectively?
- Did I honor the emotion and mood of the text?
- Did I read with sincerity? Could listeners sense that I think this passage is important?

We might consider memorizing our text. Pastors ought to set an example for the congregation in Scripture memorization anyway. Preaching a psalm gives us a good occasion to do so: they are fairly short, easier to memorize than narrative or didactic literature, and quoting from memory can be a powerful way to deliver the text.[8]

---

8 There was a time when no man could be ordained to the ministry who had not committed the entire Psalter to memory!

For Further Study

Arthurs, Jeffrey D. *Devote Yourself to the Public Reading of Scripture.* Kregel, 2012.

Bartow, Charles. *Effective Speech Communication in Leading Worship.* Abingdon, 1988.

Childers, Jana. *Performing the Word.* Abingdon, 1998.

Childers, Jana, and Clayton J. Schmit, eds. *Performance in Preaching.* Baker, 2008. Companion DVD includes performance exercises and techniques.

Jacks, G. Robert. *Getting the Word Across: Speech Communication for Pastors and Lay Leaders.* Eerdmans, 1995.

Jacks, G. Robert. *Just Say the Word: Writing for the Ear.* Eerdmans, 1996.

McComiskey, Thomas. *Reading Scripture in Public.* Baker, 1991.

McLean, Max. *Unleashing the Word: Rediscovering the Public Reading of Scripture.* Zondervan, 2009. Includes DVD with public readings and commentary by the author on each reading. Scripture index includes numerous examples from the psalms.

Rang, Jack. *How to Read the Bible Aloud.* Paulist, 1994.

Talk about It

Imagine you are planning worship at your church. Someone, a lay leader, has been asked to read a psalm. How might you advise the reader on how to get the psalm's meaning across?

Dig Deeper

View one of the DVDs included with Max McLean, *Unleashing the Word;* Jeffrey Arthurs, *Devote Yourself to the Public Reading of Scripture;* or Jana Childers and Clayton J. Schmit, eds., *Performance in Preaching.* Try out one new technique with your rendering of a psalm text.

Practice

Choose a psalm to practice reading aloud. Mark it up like this chapter suggests (or in a way that works for you) to signal suitable stresses and pauses. Practice it, then perform it, preferably for a worship service, but at least for a sympathetic critic or two. Solicit feedback on how effective your reading was.

Practice good oral delivery of your next sermon, whether or not your text is a psalm. Listen to a recording of the sermon and see if you can detect any differences in comparison to your previous preaching.

7

Emotion

Nothing illuminates the ruling passions of our hearts as dramatically or clearly as our emotions. And no book of Scripture illuminates our emotions as dramatically or clearly as the Psalms.

Dan Allender and Tremper Longman[1]

Strategy 11
Preach the Emotion of the Psalm

One mark of poetry is its unabashed appeal to our emotions. A successful poem establishes a "sympathetic contract" between writer and reader: the poet adopts an attitude toward her subject which she hopes the reader will share. If the reader misconstrues or disagrees with this emotional stance, the poem fails, even if the reader "understands" every line.[2] Biblical poems, as part of the infallible Word of God, never fail. But interpreters of biblical poems may fail. We may fail by preaching the theology, background, and valid application of the text, but not the emotional color of the text that would have strengthened the "sympathetic contract" between the biblical author and our listeners.

Biblical poets express, model, commend and command deep feeling: joy, grief, gratitude, awe, reverence, contrition, fear,

---

1 Dan B. Allender and Tremper Longman III, *The Cry of the Soul: How Our Emotions Reveal Our Deepest Questions about God* (NavPress, 1994), 25.

2 On the "sympathetic contract," see John Ciardi, *How Does a Poem Mean?* 2nd ed. (Houghton Mifflin, 1995), 205.

brokenness, elation, disappointment, loneliness, and even hatred are all evoked and expressed in relation to God. The psalmists do not merely report on their emotional experience; they invite us to make our own affective response to the reality of God, and they extend that invitation in richly emotive speech. Sermons on their psalms should attempt to do the same. We who preach psalms will try to help listeners join the psalmists in naming and learning from our shared affective experience. Together we'll explore what emotions can teach us about what's going on in our relationship to God and others.[3] If this is going to happen, we will have to learn three skills or disciplines: (1) exegeting the emotion of texts, (2) sensing what the Spirit wants us to feel in appropriating these texts, and (3) helping listeners experience the emotional dimension of texts by how we shape and deliver sermons. More briefly, we have to know it, feel it, and then say it.

"Know It" – Exegeting Emotion

In a fine book on form-sensitive preaching of the New Testament, Mike Graves says that correctly identifying the mood of a text is more important than slavishly following the structure of the text.[4] Certainly this is true when preaching the psalms. A genre-sensitive sermon *might* explicate a psalm line by line, or make good use of poetic devices, or in some other way follow the structure or imagery of the poem; but a sermon *must* reflect the poem's mood. No matter how poetically crafted a sermon might be, a mismatch between the mood of the text and the mood of the sermon would be a travesty.

Expositors who would "correctly handle the word of truth" have an obligation to attend carefully to emotions as well as ideas in poetic texts because the emotional tone of any poem is an integral part of authorial intention.[5] To miss it or misidentify it is to

---

3 This is the aim of Allender and Longman in *Cry of the Soul,* and also a large part of Eugene Peterson's project in *Answering God* (Harper, 1989).

4 Mike Graves, *The Sermon as Symphony* (Judson Press, 1997), 20.

5 "Biblical texts impart more than feelings, of course, but part of the rhetorical impact of the text, and thus its meaning, has to do with the emotional mood it creates." Thomas G. Long, *Preaching and the Literary Forms of the Bible*

misread a psalm, however accurately one might grasp the psalm's cognitive content. The same cognitive content can elicit opposite emotional responses depending on its setting in different poems. For example, in Psalm 77 the poet laments God's absence, but then he finds comfort in recalling God's faithfulness in the past.

> Then I thought, "To this I will appeal:
>   the years of the right hand of the Most High."
> I will remember the deeds of the Lord;
>   yes, I will remember your miracles of long ago.
> (Ps 77:10–11)

For another sorrowing poet, however, the idea that God was good to his people in the past only makes things worse.

> We have heard with our ears, O God;
>   our fathers have told us
> what you did in their days,
>   in days long ago. (Ps 44:1)

Once upon a time you flexed your mighty muscles and crushed our enemies. But now, alas . . .

> you have rejected and humbled us;
>   you no longer go out with our armies. (Ps 44:9)

"You made us retreat," the poem continues, "you gave us up . . . you sold us . . . all this happened though we had not forgotten you." The very same idea that brought comfort to one psalmist – that God has proven in the past how mighty he is on his people's behalf – only deepens this poet's pain because it makes their present distress even more inexplicable. For a preacher to ignore the emotional component of either of these psalms by, say, speaking of

---

(Fortress, 1989), 134. See too, Ronald Allen, *Contemporary Biblical Interpretation for Preaching* (Judson, 1984), 108. Allen suggests interpreting Scripture as a "representation of feeling," recovering the feelings which the first listeners or readers would have experienced with the language and imagery of the text.

God's faithfulness without noting the effect this theme had on the poets would be to misread them.

This is an obvious example. We can hope that no minister would preach Psalms 77 and 44 without recognizing the drastically different emotions they express. Sometimes, however, the emotional dimension of a psalm is not easy to identify, or at least not easy to identify with precision. Maybe it is obvious that a psalm expresses sorrow. But what kind of sorrow? The sorrow of contrition? The sorrow of betrayal? World-weariness? Bereavement? These feelings are not the same. Some psalmists are crushed, humbled, and plaintive in their sorrow. Others are bold, almost defiant, expecting God to make things right – now!

Let's say you are preaching Psalm 88, a lament. You may be familiar with laments, but that does not mean you have pinpointed the emotional tone of *this* lament. One commentary speaks of the poet's "agonizing scream." You agree that the psalmist is in agony, but after careful reading, it does not seem to you that his poem is a scream. He's too depressed, too weary to scream: "I am like a man without strength" (v. 4), "like the slain who lie in the grave" (v. 5); "my eyes are dim with grief " (v. 9). You try screaming these words. Then you try reading them as one who's utterly weary, one for whom speech requires effort. The latter feels truer to the poem. Perhaps if the commentator had been more attentive to the emotive connotations of this language (and it would have helped to read it aloud) he might not have misconstrued the psalm's emotion.

C.S. Lewis, usually a reliable guide to reading Scripture, misconstrued the emotion of the imprecatory psalms. He wrote of their "wickedness . . . festering, gloating, undisguised – and we should be wicked if we in any way condoned or approved it."[6]

Preachers whose view of inspiration is more conservative will hesitate to label anything in the Bible "wicked." Yet reverence for the sacred text may cause them, too, to misread emotion in the imprecatory palms. When we encounter speech that does not fit our notion of what is proper for poets writing the Bible, we may soften it, blind to how raw and intense it actually is. This is not the place to discuss Christian appropriation of the imprecatory psalms (see

---

6 C. S. Lewis, *Reflections on the Psalms* (Harcourt, 1958), 22.

a brief discussion in Appendix 1); I raise the issue here only to illustrate how preachers who struggle with strong emotion in the Psalter might misunderstand it.

Other doctrinal blinders can be a problem in exegeting the emotion of the psalms. How does our theological anthropology, for instance, impact the way we read expressions of grief and doubt in the psalms? Are these emotions "to be overcome as distractions to our life with God," or are they "the very windows through which we see the truth not merely about ourselves but also about God"?[7]

Another difficulty is that unless we are quite at home in Hebrew, some of the emotional color of the poets' language will not be apparent. Word play, cadence, and other sounds of sentences may be lost in translation. An essentially literal translation may help, preserving more of the figures of speech and formal structure of the original and thus, potentially, more of the emotional dimensions of the poem than a paraphrastic version that flattens out too much for the sake of immediate clarity. But even with a good translation or the ability to work in the original, we are far removed from the poet in time and space. The life situation behind the poem is often somewhat vague, so that the emotive color of some expressions may be a matter of conjecture. But we can at least make our conjectures more probable by patient, imaginative reading.

How to Get in Touch with the Emotion of a Text

There is no one right way to exegete the emotion of a text. Two important ways were mentioned briefly in my example of the commentator who misread Psalm 88. First, noticing the connotative value of words and sentences is non-negotiable. Then, assuming that a preacher will do at least that much, the next most valuable tool for getting in touch with the emotion of a text is probably experimenting with oral reading. Read it aloud, more than once and differently each time. "Try out" different emotions. See what feels right. Check your hunches, of course, against the content, movement, and vocabulary of the poem, and see what you learn by

---

7 J. Clinton McCann and James C. Howell *Preaching the Psalms* (Abingdon, 2001), 34–35.

comparing translations and consulting commentaries. But don't discount your intuition about which tone of voice seems to capture the affective dimension of the psalm. Try to name what the psalmist felt as precisely as possible: is it anger? bitterness? weariness? defiance? bewilderment? A lament might express any of these or more than one, but they are not identical. Is it gratitude? love? awe? relief? hope? A hymn may express any of these or more than one, but they are not the same. We should not be content with getting the emotion of our text almost right, any more than we'd be content with getting its propositional truth almost right.

Then, too, we can make responsible use of sanctified imagination. We might take time, for example, to recreate in our mind's eye the liturgical drama behind some of the psalms. These poems come alive with color and excitement in their allusions to clapping, dancing, prostration, and so on. We do not have to credit every proposed reconstruction of the cultic use of psalms in order to appreciate the obvious fact that many of them were intended for corporate worship. They were meant to be spoken, heard, and responded to by the gathered congregation. They were not meant to be read as the preacher may be reading them on a Tuesday from an easy chair.

Instead of (or in addition to) imagining the original setting, we might use our imaginations to recreate a contemporary life setting in which the psalm fits. You're reading Psalm 102, "A prayer of an afflicted man. When he is faint and pours out his lament before the Lord." As you read, you recall yesterday's visit to a hospitalized friend who is trying to maintain faith during a protracted season of suffering. Remember his weary tone, his drawn face, his tendency to fall asleep in the middle of a sentence, only to be jerked back to consciousness a moment later by a spasm of pain? Does this memory help you know how to read and speak this psalm?

Might we picture, as we read different psalms, quiet meadows or rising floods or wilderness caves, until we begin to feel what we would feel if we were actually there? Might we imagine the mood of our text in terms of color? Does it read like raging oranges or depressing grays? Garrison Keillor tells about his growing up in Lake Wobegon as a budding author who sometimes used colored pencils to write in different moods – yellow for happy thoughts, blue for sad, and so on. What color pencil might the psalmist have used to write this week's sermon text?

Some preachers try to imagine musical accompaniment to their texts.[8] Can we hear melancholy oboes as we read Psalm 88? Seventy-six trombones for the songs of the Lord's kingship? An organ belting out "A Mighty Fortress" while meditating on Psalm 46? In a sermon on Psalm 6, Calvin Swank imagined his text "sung by male voices, accompanied by double bass viol." The mood of the poem suggests ". . . the rumbling of heavy trucks, while the worshipper is at the wailing wall, offering penance for his justly punishable sins."[9]

Keeping these sounds in mind while composing sermons might go a long way toward mood-sensitive vocabulary, word pictures, and delivery. Later, when it is time to preach, we might even enlist musicians to accompany parts of the sermon. I've been impressed by the improvisational skills of organists in African-American congregations who underscore the sermon, sensitively enhancing its emotional tone.

Historical-grammatical reading of the psalms will only take a preacher so far. Karl Barth was convinced that when it comes to reading biblical stories – and I would add biblical poems – "A man without an imagination is more of an invalid than one who lacks a leg."[10] These poems make their appeal to us largely through the imagination, so we must learn to read and listen for their emotional messages with our imaginative faculties.

It is essential that we know what the poet felt many years ago – but it is not enough. A second discipline preachers need to practice is sensing what God wants us to feel today.

"Feel It" – Sensing What the Spirit Wants Us to Feel in the Text

For years my preaching was emotionally cautious. I was turned off

---

8 Graves, *Sermon as Symphony*, 20–22.

9 Calvin P. Swank, *Sermons from the Psalms* (Baker, 1962), 38.

10 Cited by John Goldingay, *Models for the Interpretation of Scripture* (Eerdmans, 1995), 38.

by emotionalism in the pulpit and made sure my own preaching was cool and rational. To tell the truth, I was suspicious of emotion in general, until Jonathan Edwards helped me see that "true religion, in great part, consists in the affections."[11] In other words, our relationship with God is supposed to be a matter of the heart; and though the biblical vocabulary for "heart" indicates something more than emotional, it is certainly not less than emotional. God not only wants us to know rightly and do rightly, he wants us to feel rightly. He commands emotions like joy (Ps 100:1; Phil 4:4; 1 Thess 5:16), hope (1 Pet 1:13), fear (Ps 2:2; Rom 11:20), peace (Col 3:15), zeal (Rom 12:11), grief (Rom 12:15; Jas 4:9), and gratitude (Pss 100:4 and 147:7; Eph 5:20). It will not do to interpret these and countless other texts as advocating behavior only – pretending to be joyful, making thankful sounds come out of your mouth whether or not you feel thankful. There's a word for this: hypocrisy.

I am no longer reluctant to engage emotion in preaching. In fact, I try to lead hearers into an authentic emotional response to the truth being preached. I believe, as Erasmus put it, that "the foremost goal of the theologian is to interpret the divine Scriptures with wisdom . . ." and to "drive out tears and to inflame hearts to heavenly things."[12] Now that I've been converted to a more biblical view of emotion, I've led my church in embracing this sentence as part of our official vision statement: "We envision well-conceived, Spirit-filled corporate worship *marked by reverent affection for the living God.*" We unapologetically aim for affective response to God and God's Word.

Of course, my people probably will not feel reverent affection for God and God's truth if I myself do not. Cicero was right: the one who would move people must himself be moved. Like Aristotle before him, he knew that rhetoric has more to do with arousing emotion in the speaker than with arousing audiences. It used to be that if I didn't feel anything about the truth I was about to preach,

11 Jonathan Edwards, *Treatise Concerning Religious Affections,* cited by John Piper in *Desiring God* (Multnomah, 1986), 219.

12 Manfred Hoffmann, *Rhetoric and Theology* (University of Toronto Press, 1994), 33.

I dismissed this lack as relatively unimportant. Sure, it would be nice to feel something rather than nothing, but if I don't, no big deal. What matters is the Truth. Nowadays, if I feel nothing about my text, I seek grace to be ashamed of myself and ask God to give me an emotion that matches what I am about to proclaim – for my own sake and for the sake of those to whom I preach.

I can do more than pray, of course. I can engage regularly in pastoral care, which helps keep preachers from becoming too bookish, too detached from the people to whom we preach. I will rejoice with those who rejoice and weep with those who weep. Then, while studying psalm texts and trying to relate them to the emotional experience of my listeners, I am more likely to ask questions like, "How does it feel to discover that your son has AIDS? To be suddenly homeless? Jobless? To get a call from the police reporting that your daughter has been assaulted?" I'll also ask, "What does it feel like to get an unexpected promotion? To learn that the suspicious spot does not show on your latest x-rays?" Fortunately, not all the emotions with which we need to identify in the psalms and in our people's lives are negative!

So, if I want to feel with my text and feel with my people, I'll do more than pray. When I do pray, I'll make sure that my praying includes praying the psalms. The spirituality of the psalms is passionate spirituality – *contagiously* passionate spirituality. Praying this literature makes preachers more passionate.

Praying the "Disciplined Passion" of the Psalms

Unfortunately, some people think "passionate" means "spontaneous" or "out of control." They read a bold, heartfelt lament, for example, and think that the psalmist simply vented his anger and hate, and that the inclusion of his poem in the Bible gives us license to do the same.

Melissa's son was killed in a car crash. She stood in her back yard and screamed her anger at God, using coarse, blasphemous profanity to tell God what she really thought of him. Later, conscience-smitten, she confessed her irreverence to a Christian counselor who reassured her that the cursing incident was part of her healing process and commended her for her psalm-like honesty.

But is this what we find in the psalms of lament? The psalmists are certainly honest, but they stop short of condemning or rejecting God.[13] When we pray their prayers with them, we do not vent; we worship. We use carefully-chosen, Spirit-given words to express boldly and honestly, but reverently, our passions before the Holy One.[14]

Remember that these compositions are finely-crafted poems. It's not as though a neighbor had a tape recorder running while the psalmist screamed whatever came to mind and then produced an unexpurgated transcript for public consumption. The psalmists reflected and then wrote; then they reflected some more and rewrote. They weighed each word, each line, struggling to say what they wanted to say, and to say it well, within the disciplined confines of Hebrew poetry. Time passed between the experience about which they prayed and the publication of their prayers.

Years ago my two youngest sons played at being poets. They would sit at the keyboard for a few minutes and whip out twenty lines of horribly forced rhymes, thinking they had produced art. (So far, none of it has been published, though it did hang on our refrigerator.) Psalms, however, *are* art, and anyone who has tried his hand at this art knows how extraordinarily difficult it is to write good poetry. The psalmists did not speak exquisite literature complete with chiasm, image, allusion, word play, rhythm, and all the other features of Hebrew poetry "off the cuff." They labored over their poem-prayers, disciplining their passion by literary craft and by what they knew of God. Their compositions were published and used publicly only after a period of reflection and editing.

---

13 I am uncomfortable with some of the language I encounter in reading about biblical lament. Some speak of the psalmists' "wholesale attack on God" or their honesty about the "abusing god." James L. Mays offers a more balanced perspective: see his *Preaching and Teaching the Psalms* (Westminster John Knox, 2006), 112.

14 Much has been written on praying the psalms, and much of it is good. But mixed into otherwise helpful treatments are instances of bad advice. For example, *A Retreat with the Psalms* by John C. Endres and Elizabeth Liebert (Paulist Press, 2001) provides ministers and laymen with fine suggestions on how to use the psalms for a period of spiritual renewal. But on page 75 we find the dubious counsel that we need to learn "the practice of unrestrained rage in prayer."

One possible and surprising result of praying the psalms may be that we discover we cannot pray them as we meant to when we started out. Kathleen Norris describes how the grandmother of a nine-year-old girl tried to assuage the child's suffering by using Psalm 109. It had been a hot afternoon, and the girl had ridden her bike to the neighborhood swimming pool to get cooled off. But she arrived as the pool was closing, and an insensitive young staff member was short with her. The granddaughter had come home in tears, and the woman suggested that they read a poem about being angry – Psalm 109. "Soon after she had entered the catalog of curses – 'Let their children be wanderers and beggars / driven from the ruins of their home. / Let creditors seize all their goods' (vv. 10–11) – the child cried out, 'Oh, stop! Stop! He's just a college kid!'"[15]

I had a similar experience. Some years ago I was forced to resign from a ministry I loved because of some ugly church politics. In the months that followed, I thought about praying the imprecations of the Psalter concerning the "bad guys" who drove me from my pastorate. I found that I could not do so. Painful though my experience was, it did not begin to compare with what David and some of his fellow poets suffered. Nor were my "enemies" anywhere near as bad as the wicked about whom the psalmists prayed such things as, "Strike them on the jaw and break their teeth!" (Ps 3:7). I did not want God to do anything of the kind, not because I am more spiritual than the psalmists, but because the people who hurt me did not merit such drastic treatment. (I did, however, pray Psalm 109:8, "May someone else take their place of leadership!")

Attempting to make the psalmists' words my own had the unanticipated result of putting my problems in perspective. I realized that if I am going to pray the stronger psalms of judgment I must do so with reference to the real moral monsters of our time. I will pray them in solidarity with my persecuted brothers and sisters around the world. And I will pray not against those who have hurt me personally, but against the enemies of Christ, who himself prayed these psalms.[16]

---

15 Kathleen Norris, "Why the Psalms Scare Us," *Christianity Today* (July 15, 1996): 20.

16 How Christians are to pray the imprecatory Psalms is a huge topic. See James E. Adams, *War Psalms of the Prince of Peace* (Presbyterian and Reformed,

Note the heading of this section: "Feel it – sensing *what the Spirit wants us to feel* in the text." What the preacher and congregation are supposed to feel is not necessarily the exact same emotion the psalmist felt, but the emotion the Holy Spirit wants us to feel as we take the psalmist's work to heart. That emotion will not be precisely the same as the psalmist's if his life was threatened by enemies and ours are not. We might feel something in harmony with him and his poem – outrage at injustice, a keen desire for God to intervene in our situation, empathy with the psalmist's fear – but it will not be identical with the poet's emotion. Nor will it be identical with the affective response of the original audience.[17]

I cannot feel for Jerusalem what the psalmists and their generation felt for Jerusalem, though I might feel something analogous about the church. I cannot feel precisely what they felt for their king, though I might feel something analogous for Jesus. As much as we have in common with the psalmists as fellow human beings and fellow believers, our emotional response to temple, sheep, sacrifice, exile, and other realities will not be identical to theirs. What matters is that we have understood their experience on an emotional level and that we resonate with this in our own reading and preaching of the psalms. Again, genre-sensitive preaching does not try to replicate the rhetorical effect of a text, but to respect and reflect it.

Say It – Preaching the Emotion of the Psalms

Having exegeted the emotion of the text and come to feel it – or an appropriate related emotion – how can preachers communicate this emotion in the pulpit? Somehow we have to: "Emotions are always stronger than ideas, and if we compel our listeners to choose between our ideas and our feelings about those ideas, they will

1991); Eugene Peterson, *Answering God,* chapter 8, "Enemies;" and Dietrich Bonhoeffer, *Psalms: The Prayer Book of the Bible* (Augsburg, 1970).

17 How we can appropriate for ourselves psalm language about literal enemies requires pastoral and theological wisdom. I think Stephen P. McCutchan displays some in *Experiencing the Psalms* (Smyth & Helwys, 2000), 31–32. He uses Psalms 17 and 27 for examples.

instinctively believe our feelings and discount the ideas."[18] The following suggestions are no substitute for the extensive homiletical literature on passion in preaching,[19] or for the freedom in delivery that comes only with maturity and experience (almost all preachers are inhibited at first), but they may help.

Trust and Use the Rhetoric of the Psalm

Students of speech have long recognized that some rhetorical devices are particularly emotive: apostrophe (addressing someone not present as if present or something not alive as if it could hear), asyndeton (omission of conjunctions, as in "government of the people, by the people, for the people"), repetition (provided it is purposeful repetition of something worth repeating), antimetabole (repetition in reverse order: "Ask not what your country can do for you, ask what you can do for your country"), understatement, overstatement, and others.[20]

Some of these figures and tropes occur in psalm texts. Why not use them? The parallel repetition with which the poet starts Psalm 55, for instance:

Listen to my prayer, O God,
    do not ignore my plea;
    hear me and answer me.

Hebrew synonymous parallelism always involves some kind of repetition, but this line is a tricolon, less common in the Psalter than the typical bicolon line and so more noticeably, deliberately

---

18 Dwight E. Stevenson and Charles F. Diehl, *Reaching People from the Pulpit* (Baker, 1958), 54.

19 See almost any basic homiletics text or book on sermon delivery; more to the point, Robin Meyers, *With Ears to Hear* (The Pilgrim Press, 1993); Stevenson and Diehl, *Reaching People from the Pulpit,* Richard F. Ward, *Speaking from the Heart: Preaching with Passion* (Abingdon, 1990), Henry H. Mitchell, *Celebration and Experience in Preaching* (Abingdon, 1990).

20 Jane Blankenship, *Public Speaking: A Rhetorical Perspective* (Prentice-Hall, 1966), 75; William H. Kooienga, *Elements of Style for Preaching* (Zondervan, 1989), particularly chapters 10 and 12.

repetitive. Whatever else the preacher may do to honor the poem-ness of Psalm 55, this at least should be done: restate the petition, "God, hear our prayer." Say it several times: if the psalmist says it three times in a poem that takes ninety seconds to read, how many times might the preacher say it in a twenty-five minute sermon so that listeners feel its evocative power?

"Oh," sighs the poet in Psalm 53:6, "Oh, that salvation for Is-rael would come out of Zion!" Oh, what emotion is in that "Oh!" Trust it. Use it. "Oh, that our Lord's return might be soon. Oh, that the day might come when innocent children are no longer caught in random drive-by shootings. Oh, that scoundrels might not win election to high office. Oh, that the kingdom might come at last." If starting a sentence with "Oh" would seem dated or odd in a giv-en congregation, the preacher can surely find some contemporary, culturally appropriate way to voice and evoke deep longing. In the field of communication studies, the use of sound effects and par-ticles is called "paralanguage"; things like, "Hmm," "whew," and "ugh." These convey a lot of emotion, are extremely efficient, and communicate for the ear.

Often, however, we can use what the poet has given us. We will not just say what the psalmist says; we will say it like the psalmist says it. Since poems are intentionally affective, trusting their use of language makes sense in a sermon that seeks to move people emotionally. Everything in chapter 4 about using the psalm's poet-ic devices or English substitutes applies here, especially those de-vices that move listeners emotionally. But one feature of poetry in particular deserves special attention: hyperbole.

Do Not be Afraid of Hyperbole

Hyperbole is the language of strong feeling. It is the speech of the oppressed and the ecstatic. It is the language of those for whom ordinary speech is inadequate. Hyperbole may not stand up to logical scrutiny, but then the speaker does not intend it to. Such language, whether hyperbolic praise or hyperbolic lament, helps us express deeply felt emotion.

"My bones wasted away through my groaning all day long" (Ps 32:3) is not a statement verifiable in the doctor's office, but it is truthful praying. "Why, O Lord, do you stand far off? Why do you hide yourself?" (Ps 10:1) is not a challenge to the doctrine of God's omnipresence, but an expression of the sufferer's sense of abandonment. "How long, O Lord?" (Ps 6:3) is not a request for information, but a plea to be heard. "He drew me out of deep waters . . . he brought me into a spacious place" (Ps 18:16, 19) may not be literally true for us, yet still express truthfully our experience of divine deliverance. "You turned my wailing into dancing" (Ps 30:11) is a prayer I can pray even though, klutz that I am, I stay far away from the dance floor.

Voicing these hyperbolic phrases may help both preacher and congregation evoke, name, recognize, own, affirm, or repent of what we feel because hyperbole enlarges an idea or emotion and says, "Notice this!" Not all of us are good at noticing and articulating what we think and feel. Using the good strong words of God's word may help us when otherwise the right words will not come.

When David prays, "Against you, you only have I sinned" (Ps 51:4), he uses a kind of hyperbole, for surely he has sinned against Bathsheba and Uriah and, indeed, against his whole nation. But when he prays this way, and when we make his words our own, we are brought to the realization that ultimately sin has more to do with God than with other people. When we make Asaph's hyperbolic statement our own, "I was a brute beast before you" (Ps 73:22), we realize in the speaking what he came to realize: how stupid it is to envy the wicked.

Of course, no speech, however well-crafted, can guarantee affective, imaginative, and aesthetic response. Rhetoric is not an exact science. It deals in probabilities.[21] So a sermon must be more than preacherly emoting. It cannot be all hyperbole, or one figure of speech after another. A blend of emotionally evocative rhetoric and clear propositional content will be more effective than either alone.

---

21 Carroll C. Arnold, *Criticism of Oral Rhetoric* (Charles E. Merrill, 1974), 15.

Preach Out of the Depths

"Out of the depths I cry to you, O Lord," says the anonymous song of ascent, Psalm 130. Has the preacher ever so preached or prayed publically as to let people know they can pray out of the depths? Or has the contemporary church's obsession with the positive, the upbeat, the celebratory closed off this possibility for the congregation? Here's a thought experiment for pastors: Suppose someone in your church died in a tragic accident. Would you expect to see the family in church the following Sunday, or does everyone assume they will take a few weeks off? Honest wrestling with this question might tell you something about congregational culture as it relates to the legitimacy of lament. Do people think of church as a safe place to be sad?

I recall a cartoon I saw in a ministry journal years ago. God must have known I needed it because he burned it into my consciousness. A pastor (who could be me) is preaching; above his head is a thought balloon in which he fancies himself a general, helmet and all, leading the congregational army out to do battle. "Charge!" he cries. But over the heads of the congregation is a different thought balloon: they see themselves lying on the battlefield, desperately wounded. "Medic!" they cry. Our pews are filled with people who are crushed by life; people loaded down with guilt they do not know what to do with; people angry at God; people engaged in denial because they think it is unspiritual to talk about their pain.

It may be important, in a day when praise is confused with happiness, and worship with the upbeat, to realize that the sadder emotions are acknowledged in the psalms. Preachers would do well to mull over Walter Brueggemann's words and not hesitate to preach laments:

> The use of these "psalms of darkness" . . . is an act of faith. . . .
> it insists that all such experiences of disorder are a proper subject for discourse with God. There is nothing out of bounds, nothing precluded or inappropriate. Everything properly belongs in this conversation of the heart. To withhold parts of life

from that conversation is in fact to withhold part of life from the sovereignty of God. Thus these psalms make the important connection; everything must be *brought to speech*, and everything must be *addressed to God*, who is the final reference for all of life.[22]

Brueggemann and others have called for a recovery of lament in the church for some time now. I do not know whether this call is being heeded or not, but I do know that a lot of churches call their worship hour a "celebration service." Why? Is celebration the only emotion we are permitted to express in corporate worship? Has anyone started a weekly "lament service," scheduled, perhaps, in the wee hours of the morning when the targeted market niche can't sleep anyway?

Half of the psalms are laments. That's too much material for a preacher to ignore simply because the culture currently prefers celebration. It is true that almost all laments include a turn to praise; but as Emily Dickinson put it, "Pain – is missed – in Praise"[23] Pain is not denied, suppressed or delegitimized; it is caught up – all in good time, and after honest experience – and *then* "lost" in praise.

One way a preacher can handle the emotion of a lament honestly is to not be in a hurry to "get to the good stuff." One of my students, preaching Psalm 73, told us in the sermon's introduction where we would end up – in a place of confident orthodoxy, secure with God as our all-satisfying treasure. This was a mistake. I do not mean it was a mistake to conclude the sermon that way, but it was a mistake to introduce it that way. Although the student did walk us through the poet's doubts in the first movement of the psalm, this part of the sermon lacked conviction since the preacher had given away the happy ending. During our debrief time, I pointed out that the poet arrives where he does only after honest wrestling with the prosperity of the wicked, and that perhaps the sermon, too, might let listeners feel this struggle a bit longer before resolving the tension. The student agreed. He had thought about it when

22 Walter Brueggemann, *The Message of the Psalms* (Fortress, 1984), 52.
23 Poem #18, also known as "Unto my books so good to turn," *The Complete Poems of Emily Dickenson* (Little, Brown, and Company, 1924), 74.

writing the sermon but was afraid to let listeners squirm for more than a minute or two with the kind of pained speech we encounter in this psalm.[24]

Genre-sensitive preachers will not be afraid to let listeners squirm. We will preach out of the depths. But neither will we fail to preach the joy which is, after all, the final and pervasive emotional note of the Psalter.

Let Them Hear the Angels Sing

James Howell recalls his first experience preaching in an African American church. He feared that his sermon would seem pretty bland after the exuberant time of worship, especially when the pastor introduced him: "Brother Howell, come now, unfurl for us the scroll of heaven so that we might hear the angels sing."[25]

"Unfurl the scroll of heaven so we can hear the angels sing" – not a bad description of what the preacher is often privileged to do when preaching the psalms. "Shout for joy to the Lord." "Clap your hands, all you nations." "Praise the Lord from the heavens, praise him in the heights above. Praise him all his angels, praise him, all his heavenly hosts." "Let everything that has breath praise the Lord." How can we even think about preaching such lines matter-of-factly? Somehow, joy must come through in word choice and facial expression and tone of voice. Anglo or Asian or Latino preachers will not want to mimic an African-American homiletical tradition that is foreign to them; that would come off as cheesy. But we must find our own authentic celebratory voice so that God's people can hear the angels sing.

Emotions like joy and awe are communicated not only by tone of voice, but by energetic words, sentences, and paragraphs put together with "style." I once heard a preacher try to wow a congregation with astronomical data that illustrated the grandeur of God. We were supposed to be moved by the greatness of the Creator,

---

24 McCann and Howell offer sound advice on not short-circuiting the listener's experience of lament by premature movement to sermonic resolution of tension: *Preaching the Psalms,* 77.

25 McCann and Howell, *Preaching the Psalms,* 126

but the information was so detailed and read so pedantically, it just didn't work. Briefer statements of fewer facts, with Psalm sentences interspersed, perhaps, would have worked better:

> *Did you know that the Milky Way is but one of a hundred billion galaxies swimming with stars? That only one other galaxy is close enough to see with the naked eye – a smudge of light in the night sky, yet twice the size of our galaxy and home to a trillion stars? "O Lord, our Lord, how majestic is your name in all the earth!" Did you know that if our eyes were strong enough to see them all, a dime held at arm's length would block out fifteen million stars from view? And that many of them dwarf our sun? If Antares stood where our sun stands – ninety-three million miles away – we'd be inside it. "What is man that you are mindful of him?"*

More could be said, and in greater detail, but this is a sermon, not a scientific paper. The information should be used to inspire awe. So explanation is minimized. We don't have to spell it out for people that "Antares" is a star; they can figure that out from the context. We don't have to say, "This is why the psalmist is amazed that God pays attention to us puny humans." That connection is clear. No word wax is needed here – no footnotes, no citation of sources, no expository prose that bogs down the imaginative power of the illustration. Just say it.

Let Your Emotion Show – to a Point

Somewhere I read that when Abraham Lincoln went to church he liked to see the preacher flailing his arms "as if he were fighting bees." He wanted to sense that the message mattered to the preacher.

Flailing arms would be off-putting in my congregation, so some other contextually appropriate gesture, tone of voice, vocabulary or posture must convey intensity. Like every preacher, I have to find my own way to communicate emotion authentically. Jonathan Edwards didn't flail. In fact, he gestured very little. But those who heard him preach were affected by "... overwhelming weight of argument, and with such intenseness of feeling, that the whole soul of the speaker is thrown into every part of the conception and delivery."[26] It is worth repeating that "weight of argument" and "intenseness of feeling" are not to opposed to one another. As noted in an earlier chapter, Edwards stated that his aim was "... to raise the affections of my hearers as high as I possibly can, *provided they are affected with nothing but the truth,* and, with affections that are not disagreeable to the nature of what they are affected with" [emphasis added].

Finding the right way to express weight of argument and intenseness of feeling calls for pastoral sensitivity. We have to know our people and the local culture. We have to be ourselves. Sometimes just a touch of emotion in the pulpit is all that's needed, like a dash of lemon juice in the apple pie. But I am inclined to agree with Spurgeon that "even fanaticism is to be preferred to indifference."[27]

For Further Study

Mitchell, Henry. *Celebration and Experience in Preaching.* Abingdon, 1990.

Allender, Dan B. and Tremper Longman, *Cry of the Soul: How Our Emotions Reveal Our Deepest Questions About God.* NavPress, 1994.

NOTE: Standard works on classical rhetoric can help you identify modes of speech that move listeners emotionally. Many homiletics texts include delivery advice for expressing authentic pathos. But if you want to preach psalms emotively, there is no substitute for reading them carefully, exegeting their emotions, and then praying that God will help you feel what you ought to feel when you preach them. Authentic emotion will be "caught" more than "taught" by rhetorical techniques.

---

26 Sereno Dwight, *Memoirs,* in *The Works of Jonathan Edwards* (repr.; Banner of Truth, 1974), l:cxc.

27 Charles Haddon Spurgeon, *An All-Round Ministry* (Banner of Truth, 1990), 173.

Talk about It

Read aloud two lament psalms (you might consider Pss 6, 17, 22, 64, or 69) and identify as precisely as possible the dominant emotion of each. "Sadness" is not specific enough; is it bitter sadness, angry sadness, sadness colored by hope? Something else? What could a preacher do to communicate this emotion in a sermon on the psalm?

Dig Deeper

Think about the use of psalms in other kinds of ministries of the Word: pastoral counseling, for example. See Ken Langley, "Genre-Sensitive Counseling from the Psalms," *Journal of Biblical Counseling*, 20, no. 3 (Spring 2002): 38–45; and "Praying Poetry," *Journal of Biblical Counseling*, 21, no. 2 (Winter 2003): 28–36.

Practice

Consider someone you trust and who will give you honest feedback on your next sermon. Ask them to read this chapter so they can informatively evaluate the use of emotion in your next sermon.

8

Context

The Psalter is the book of all saints; and everyone, in whatever situation he may be, finds in that situation Psalms and words that fit his case, that suit him as if they were put there just for his sake, so that he could not put it better himself, or find or wish for anything better.[1]
Martin Luther

Strategy 12
Preach the Psalm in Its Literary Context

For a long time, the Psalter was considered a haphazardly organized song book. Unlike contemporary hymnals, which are helpfully arranged by topic, the ordering of the psalms seemed to display neither rhyme nor reason. This perception of randomness is understandable: we do not find sections on "creation hymns" or "Torah psalms" or "wisdom poems." Laments are not lumped together (though they are more frequent in the first half of the Psalter); praise songs are not collected in one section (though praise becomes the dominant note toward the end of the book).

For those who, like millions of believers down through the centuries, are committed to life-long reading of the psalms sequentially, this varied arrangement is a blessing. Not only is variety inherently interesting, but the shifts of mood, theme, and style in the Psalter mirror real life, where circumstances change unpredictably.

---

1 "Preface to the Psalter," *Luther's Works* (Fortress, 1960), 35:255–56.

If randomness in the psalms was the whole story, there would be little homiletical significance to a psalm's location in the collection. A preacher could treat each text as a stand-alone literary unit, much as if he or she was preaching a verse from the book of Proverbs. Recently, however, scholars have begun to notice a degree of purposeful ordering in the Psalter. Psalms 1 and 2 are now widely regarded as a strategically-paired introduction, emphasizing the two central concerns of Israel's worship, Torah and the reign of Yahweh. Psalms 146 through 150 seem a fitting conclusion, given the Hebrew title for the book, "Praises." Although there are more laments than hymns in the Psalter, praise does end up coloring all that's gone before, not only by the higher percentage of hymns in the second half of the book, but by this rousing five-psalm call to praise at the end of the collection.

Sermons on the first and second psalms may want to take into account the theological weight they carry as an introduction to the collection. Sermons on the final Hallelujah psalms may want to include a sense of retrospect, of having "gotten to" these songs by way of a longer, varied spiritual journey. Certainly any *series* on the psalms should display the book's progression and theological coherence. A series on the whole collection might take the congregation on an honest but hopeful journey that moves from lament to praise. All hundred and fifty would not have to be preached, but a sampling that includes each of the major types of psalms over several weeks could still give listeners a new appreciation for Psalms as a book.

In between the introductory pair and the concluding set there is further evidence of purposeful groupings of psalms. Psalm 7 ends with David's intention to praise the Lord; Psalm 9 begins with that same resolution; and Psalm 8 embodies what he says he will do in the other two. Psalms 7 and 9 are laments; Psalm 8 is the first song of praise in the Psalter. Is it coincidental that this hymn is sandwiched between two prayers for deliverance? Given the interplay of praise and lament in the book as a whole, this grouping appears to be paradigmatic—and homiletically suggestive as well. Preachers will want to handle laments in light of praise and praise in light of lament. The lament we commend is honest yet hopeful.

The praise we commend is voiced with brokenhearted joy. Psalms 15 through 24 may be read as a set whose first and last poems form a chiasm on who may enter God's presence and how. Psalms 96 to 99 (with 93) are known as "Hymns of the Lord's Kingship," a set that may be preached as such. Psalms 103 and 104 appear to be intentionally paired: both begin and end with "Praise the Lord, O my soul," an expression found only here in the psalms. Psalms 113 through 118 share some common themes and a setting as praise songs of the Passover liturgy.[2] The long historical Psalms 105 and 106 close the fourth book of the Psalter, followed by Psalm 107, which introduces the final book with a different kind of narrative. Here the story of God's steadfast love for his people plays out not on the grand scale of national sin and salvation as in 105 and 106, but in vignettes of ordinary people in peril. A genre-sensitive preacher who is aware of these pairings and groupings might ask, "How should a sermon on this psalm take special note of its literary context?"

Psalm 120 through 134, the songs of ascent, were sung by pilgrims on their way to worship in Jerusalem. Though they are individual poems, commonalities and a sense of progress from one to the next enrich our understanding of all of them. If these fifteen Psalms were meant to be read and chanted in light of each other, may there not be good reason for preaching them in this way? If here or elsewhere in the Psalter we discover purposeful placement of psalms in proximity to one another, and if this arrangement is a dimension of divine inspiration or providential canonization, it is genre-sensitive and theologically responsible for preachers to honor the surrounding context of their psalm texts, perhaps by preaching a short series on a selection of these songs of ascent.

Examples could be multiplied of how scholars are now trying to read the Psalter as a coherent book.[3] Some find "stitch words,"

---

2 In addition to shared theme and liturgical setting, Mays and others see development from psalm to psalm in this grouping. James L. Mays, *Preaching and Teaching the Psalms* (Westminster John Knox, 2006), 38.

3 Patrick Miller summarizes the case for reading the psalms as a book in "The Psalter as a Book of Theology," in *Psalms in Community*, ed. Harold W. Attridge and Margot Fassler (Society of Biblical Literature, 2003), 87–98. His bibliographic notes will refer students to several other key scholars who advocate

linking a psalm with its neighbors. Others are attentive to the "seams" of the book, the placement of wisdom and royal psalms at important junctures, or the pivotal position of Psalm 73 at the beginning of "Book 3," signaling, perhaps, a turn from lament to praise in Israel's experience of God. Some, like Gerald Wilson, look for evidence of "frames" imposed on the collection by editors interested in eschatology or the Davidic kingship or wisdom or all of the above.[4]

Precisely how and when the Psalter arrived at its current shape and according to what editorial policies are still matters of speculation; consensus on these questions may never be achieved. Accordingly, this strategy of contextual reading and preaching is offered with a word of caution: while evidence for intentionality in grouping smaller sets of psalms is strong, proposals regarding the arrangement of the entire Psalter must be regarded as tentative and provisional. The preacher need not wait for consensus on the macrostructure of the Psalter before handling *some* psalms with sensitivity to their literary context.[5]

Eugene Peterson's *A Long Obedience in the Same Direction,* for example, skillfully exposits the songs of ascent (Pss 120–134) and demonstrates how a preacher might handle a series on this or another of the Psalter's sub-groupings.[6] When these psalms are read

---

this approach in different ways. Norman Whybray is skeptical of any claim that the Psalter as a whole was purposefully shaped as a book. *Reading the Psalms as a Book* (Sheffield Academic Press, 1996).

4 For an accessible summary of this kind of research, see Wilson's chapter, "The Structure of the Psalter," in *Interpreting the Psalms,* ed. David Firth and Philip S. Johnston (IVP, 2005), and David Howard's chapter, "The Psalms and Current Study" in the same volume.

5 Though Norman Whybray doubts that the Psalter as a whole was purposefully shaped as a book, he agrees that thematic and (maybe) "catchword" linking of pairs and small group of psalms is evident. If he is right, and few would dispute this, the observation has homiletical significance. *Reading the Psalms as a Book* (Sheffield Academic Press, 1996), 121. Tremper Longman, too, remains unconvinced that the Psalter evidences a comprehensive unifying structure: "From Weeping to Rejoicing," chapter 15 in *The Psalms: Language for All Seasons of the Soul,* ed. Andrew Schmutzer and David M. Howard (Moody Press, 2013).

6 Eugene H. Peterson, *A Long Obedience in the Same Direction* (InterVarsity, 1980).

together under the metaphor of pilgrimage, the whole means more than the sum of the parts.

Psalm 23 can be read and preached in light of Psalm 22: the Good Shepherd died with Psalm 22's cry of dereliction on his lips; so whatever it means to walk through the valley of the shadow of death, fearing no evil, it does not mean that we are guaranteed immunity from deep and painful suffering any more than Jesus was. This insight helped Martin Luther preach Psalm 23 honestly. He wondered aloud how God could allow him to be so plagued by terrors and doubts: "When will He ever begin to manifest in me that He is my shepherd?"[7]

The pronouncement of blessing at the beginning of Psalm 1 and the end of Psalm 2 may be seen as an envelope structure signaling God's approval on Torah-lovers and on all who take refuge in his anointed king. The *inclusio* demonstrates that these are not two blessings but one, not two groups of people but one. Preaching either psalm, we might want to note that contextual insight and what it implies for the way listeners understand the poem and what it implies for the way we read the rest of the Psalter.

Not every psalm has a literary context, but we should be alert to the possibility. Some psalms can be faithfully preached without explicit reference to neighboring poems, but the theological context of Israel's book of songs and prayers will never be far from the mind of the genre-sensitive expositor.

And then there's another context to be considered: the context of corporate worship in which most sermons are preached.

Strategy 13
Plan Other Aspects of the Worship Service to Maximize Listeners' Experience of the Psalm

Not for the first time the reader may wonder, "Why is *this* being proposed as a *genre-sensitive* strategy for the psalms?" Like paying attention to words (strategy #8), or practicing sermons aloud (#9), placing the sermon in the context of a worship service that

---

7 Martin Luther, *Selections from the Psalms*, Luther's Works, ed. J. Pelikan (Concordia, 1955), 12:159.

maximizes our experience of the text seems like a good idea no matter what genre we're preaching. Shouldn't preachers routinely collaborate with other worship leaders to create services that flow smoothly from prelude to postlude, each element of the service reinforcing the others? (If any Ministers of Music are reading this book, there might be wistful sighing or rueful laughter at this point!)

Certainly this and some of the other strategies fit other types of biblical literature as well. But this strategy seems to me particularly appropriate for preaching the psalms because psalms were made for corporate worship. They practically beg to be prayed, chanted, sung, or shouted. They *want* to be used for responsive readings, offertory sentences, calls to worship, confessions and benedictions. No part of the Bible presents the liturgist with better material than the psalms.

So the preacher's psalm could be put to good use prior to or after the sermon. If the text is read before the sermon, then at the very least it should be read well (everything in chapter six regarding skillful oral interpretation applies here). Additional suggestions include reading the psalm more than once from different translations, inviting a well-rehearsed choral reading group to read or quote the psalm, perhaps with simple choreography that does not distract from the text but accentuates its movement.[8]

There are other ways to use the sermon text in worship. On a morning he preached Psalm 145, a pastor began the service seated with the congregation. After the prelude, he stood and, without introduction, recited the psalm from memory as a call to worship. He moved toward the pulpit as he spoke, his delivery of the psalm more intense with each step up to the platform and with each repetition of the psalm's thematic word "all." "The Lord is righteous in *all* his ways and loving toward *all* he has made. The Lord is near to *all* who call on him," and so on. Therefore, "Let *every* creature praise his holy name for ever and ever." At these words the organ

---

8 See Jeffrey D. Arthurs, *Devote Yourself to the Public Reading of Scripture* (Kregel, 2012), chapter 7 on group reading; Gordon C. Bennett, *Reader's Theater Comes to Church* (Merriweather, 1985), and numerous internet resources for church drama.

introduced "All Creatures of Our God and King," and the congregation did what the psalm told them to do. Later, the psalm's assurances of divine provision were included in the offertory prayer, and its final exhortation to praise the Lord was repeated at the end of the service in place of a normal benediction. So the psalm was used at least three other times during the service in addition to the sermon. The congregation went home that day having experienced Psalm 145.

On that occasion, the sermon came where it usually comes for many of us, near the end of the service. But on a different Lord's Day, I heard a psalm preached at the beginning of worship. Psalm 24 is an entrance liturgy, and the preacher wisely chose to preach it early on and then let the congregation do what the poet and preacher urge them to do – open the gates of their hearts that the King of Glory may come in. The sermon was followed by an extended time of joyful singing and other elements of worship. I know this preacher. He likes to vary the order of service anyway. But in this instance he was being deliberately genre-sensitive: the placement of the sermon matched the rhetorical intent of the psalm.

Similarly, a sermon on a penitential psalm might introduce a time of individual and corporate confession. A sermon on a thanksgiving psalm might be capped by a testimony from someone in the congregation whose experience echoes the psalmist's. A sermon on a lament might lead into an extended time of intercessory prayer. After I preached Psalm 88, a soloist accompanied by a single plaintive flute sang "Come, Ye Disconsolate, Where're Ye Languish," as hurting congregants made their way to the front of the sanctuary to pray with others. The poet's honest lament had given them permission to pour out their heart to God. The service ended with an oral prayer—by someone I had coached to pray in a tone that would not clash with that of the psalm and sermon.

If the congregation receives a worship folder or bulletin, this handout can include explanatory notes on the psalm – the kind of material preachers want people to know but which bog down a sermon and make it too much like a lecture. The bulletin might also feature quotations: C.S. Lewis called Psalm 19 "one of the greatest lyrics in the world," or "Spurgeon said our text this morning, Psalm

131, is 'quick to read but long to learn.'" Perhaps the Psalm itself might be featured on the cover of the folder, rendered by a church member skilled in calligraphy. Or the church secretary could shop in advance (given adequate lead time by the preacher!) for a bulletin cover with professional artwork appropriate for the psalm. Maybe a version of the psalm in English poetry could be included in the bulletin (and/or read aloud in the service); excellent sources include metrical psalm collections for corporate singing, *The Poet's Book of Psalms,* and other poetry collections referenced in chapter four.

Musical Settings of the Sermon Text

Speaking of metrical Psalters, do not forget to sing the sermon text! Psalms have been set to a wide variety of musical styles. For a sermon text that exalts God as our Rock, there's "Rock of Ages," "A Mighty Fortress," "Ain't No Rock," maybe even Stryper's signature song, "The Rock That Makes Us Roll" (though I'm not sure I'd recommend Stryper for most worship services!). It might be possible to sing the psalm of the day two or three times in different versions. Some settings are easy to learn, even for congregations that do not routinely use a metrical Psalter. For more difficult arrangements, a choral anthem, a solo, or taped music may be options for maximizing the congregation's exposure to the sermon text. Again, this may seem like nothing new to worship planners who work hard at unified themes every week: selecting music that echoes the sermon text just makes sense. But the case for musical expression of psalm sermon texts is particularly strong: these texts were meant to be sung. Their poetic power can only be enhanced when they are both preached and sung.[9]

What use might worship planners make of liturgical dance? Or the visual arts? Our church has a hundred-year-old tradition of selecting a "watch word" for the year, a theme verse announced by the pastor on New Year's Eve and referred to throughout the year. One year when I preached through the life and psalms of David,

---

9 Among the helpful sources of musical and other material on Psalms is the web site of Crown and Covenant Publications, www.Psalms4u.com.

our watch word was Psalm 65:1, "Praise awaits you, O God, in Zion" (especially apt for Christ Community Church in *Zion,* Illinois). Near the beginning of the year, artist Tim Botts did a calligraphic rendering of this text during our morning worship service. While he sketched, he spoke of what the verse meant to him and how his visual rendition of it was meant to "work." He later made a finished version of the piece, which now hangs in our building.

Help from Other Psalms

We do not have to limit ourselves to the sermon text when planning a worship experience that maximizes the impact of a psalm. Other psalms may fit the bill. Perhaps the preacher does not want to give away too much by praying Psalm 51 before he preaches it, so a different penitential Psalm is used for the congregation's confession of sin. Maybe the sermon text is Psalm 97; this psalm does not say anything about worship through giving material offerings to God—but Psalm 96 does. And since these songs of the Lord's kingship are closely related by theme as well as proximity, it is natural to borrow Psalm 96:8, "Bring an offering and come into his courts," when planning a service around Psalm 97. Or if the preacher's text is Psalm 95, the worship planner might use the opening verse of Psalm 96: "Sing to the Lord a new song; sing to the Lord, all the earth."

Themes running through the Psalter include God as rock or fortress, enemies, the beauty of holiness, the treasure we have in Torah, God's sovereignty over creation, the certainty that God will answer prayer, the joyful duty of delighting in him and, more specifically, of praising him in music and song. If the psalm sermon text for the morning touches one of these themes, how about a dramatic reading of selections from other psalms on the same theme?

While writing this chapter I attended a service where the sermon text was Psalm 73. Virtually all of the congregational singing that day was from psalm texts (and this is not a congregation that limits itself to singing only the canonical psalms). I think the worship leader overlooked some selections which would have matched the preacher's text better, but simply singing a lot of psalms helped immerse worshippers into the world of the Psalter – a good way to lead up to the preaching moment.

Now and then a student will ask me, "How much time do you spend preparing a sermon?" My normal answer is that it's hard to say because I do not prepare sermons, I plan worship services that include sermons. I think about music, Scripture readings, prayers, dramatic vignettes, and the "arc" of the service, all of which is meant to work with the sermon as a unified package. I commend this way of planning to my homiletics classes, especially with reference to preaching psalms.

If the reader wonders whether this particular strategy deserves special mention as a strategy for the psalms, the next is likely to evoke the same reservations.

Strategy 14
Preach Psalms on Special
Occasions and in Timely Series

Few preachers will have the desire to preach the whole book of Psalms sequentially or the skill to sustain congregational interest for such a long series. Fortunately, faithfulness to the nature and message of the Psalter is not as dependent on sequential exposition as is the case with some books of the Bible. In fact, the psalms lend themselves to occasional preaching.

Special Occasions

Their poetic character makes them particularly appropriate for moments or seasons in the church's life where affective, imaginative, and aesthetic impact is likely to be appreciated. Thanks to their affective power, they are well-suited to tender moments, which is why we instinctively turn to psalms for funerals. Thanks to their imaginative power, they are just right for times when the church need a fresh vision of God, which is why many preachers turned to the psalms following the 2001 terrorist attacks. Thanks to their aesthetic appeal, they are well-suited to grand, celebratory moments in the life of the church, which is why we may turn to the Psalter for new beginnings, dedications, send-offs, or commissionings. "Beauty," the sermon by James Howell mentioned in chapter one, marked the anniversary of the building of a beautiful sanctuary. Howell found the exalted language of the psalms particularly well-suited to a service celebrating beauty.

It's Thanksgiving; the pastor turns to Psalm 103 ("Praise the Lord, O my soul, and forget not all his benefits") or Psalm 65 ("You crown the year with your bounty"). The congregation moves into a new facility; on their first of many Sundays in this sacred space, the pastor preaches Psalm 15 ("Lord, who may dwell in your sanctuary?"). A musician joins the church staff; the pastor preaches Psalm 96 on the essence of worship and the importance of congregational song ("Sing to the Lord a new song," and "Ascribe to the Lord the glory due his name"). Local churches have gathered for prayer in the aftermath of a horrendous crime; the speaker for the evening preaches a community lament (perhaps Psalm 12, "Help, Lord, for the godly are no more"). It's Memorial Day, a fitting occasion to affirm soldiering as a God-honoring vocation; the preacher exposits Psalm 144 ("Praise be to the Lord, my Rock, who trains my hands for war"). Or, maybe, the nation's militaristic mood calls, instead, for a sermon on Psalm 20 ("Some trust in chariots and some in horses, but we trust in the name of the Lord our God"). The psalms lend themselves to occasional preaching—and to preaching series.

Series

Perhaps the minister wants to teach a biblical theology of creation. The teaching will take place not in a classroom, but in corporate worship. To keep the instruction doxological in tone and not overly didactic, the preacher might turn to psalms describing God's lordship over the world (Pss 8, 19, 24, 29, 65, 98, 104, and 148, for example) for a series entitled "All Creatures of Our God and King."

Maybe the pastor needs a fresh approach to preaching in December. A series on psalms alluded to in Advent songs and Christmas carols might fit the bill: Psalm 24 ("Lift Up Your Heads, Ye

Mighty Gates"), any of the messianic psalms ("Come, Thou Long-Expected Jesus,"), and of course Psalms 96 and 98 ("Joy to the World"). A sermon on Psalm 2 might prepare worshippers to sing "Once in Royal David's City," "What Child Is This?" or "The Birthday of a King" without the sentimentality so common at Christmas time and with fresh appreciation of the sovereign majesty of Him whose birthday we mark.

And what about the weeks preceding Easter? As someone put it, "The Psalms were made for Lent."[10] Penitential psalms, hallowed by centuries of use by the people of God, enable us to voice our confession and confidence in God's mercy revealed supremely on the cross. And of course Psalm 22, quoted by our Lord in his cry of dereliction, would also fit such a series.

Do our people know that they can be open before God in pain and brokenness? How about a series, "Too Honest to Play Pious," on the psalms of lament? Does the church need instruction on how to pray? How about a series that includes titles like "Angry Prayer" (Ps 94), "Despairing Prayer" (Ps 88), "Joyful Prayer" (Ps 66), "Grateful Prayer" (Ps 65), and so on. After all, the Psalter is *the* canonical prayer book for the people of God. Such a sermon series might be supplemented by a study in adult education classes of any number of books on praying psalms.[11]

Does the congregation know of God's heart for the nations? One church chose Psalm 96:3 for its week-long missions conference theme: "Declare His Glory Among the Nations." Nightly reports from mission partners left no time for fully-developed sermons, but each evening included a brief devotional from one or more psalms emphasizing the global vision and missionary heart of God. Psalms 2, 48, 67, 87, 96, 98, 99, 110, 117, and 145 might work well for a missions sermon series.

---

10 Robert G. McCreight, *The Psalms Were Made for Lent* (CSS Publishing, 1996); his six sermons and worship services are not on the penitentials.

11 See Dietrich Bonhoeffer, *Psalms: The Prayer Book of the Bible* (Augsburg, 1974); John Endres and Elizabeth Liebert, *A Retreat with the Psalms* (Paulist, 2001); Stanley L. Jaki, *Praying the Psalms* (Eerdmans, 2001); Eugene H. Peterson, *Answering God: The Psalms as Tools for Prayer* (HarperCollins, 1989); Walter Brueggemann, *Praying the Psalms* (St. Mary's Press, 1982); James Sire, *Learning to Pray Through the Psalms* (IVP, 2005).

Other series might include Messiah in the Psalms, Images of Salvation in the Psalms, Sickness and Healing in the Psalms, A Thirst for God, The Way of Wisdom, The Transforming Power of Praise, War Psalms of the Prince of Peace (an exploration of the imprecatory Psalms),[12] Meet the God Who Writes Poetry, For Those Who Sin and Those Who are Sinned Against, Jesus Prays the Psalms, David and the Psalms, The Choirmaster's Favorites, and much more. There are inexhaustible riches in the Psalter—plenty to keep a preacher busy over decades of pulpit ministry.

Most printed collections of sermons on the psalms that I have seen are not united by a common theme; they are simply a few of the author's favorites. And why not? Although there are other ways to decide what to preach – the lectionary, the needs of the congregation, the season of the year, circumstances in the community – many preachers find that the most effective sermons are those they preach because they are excited about them. God has spoken to them through a text, and they want to pass it on.

There may be times—in between other, longer series, or when the preacher realizes that it is time to do something from the Old Testament—when a series of personal favorites from the psalms feels just right. Summer might be such a time. Attendance is spotty, so a series that relies on unbroken continuity might be better saved till fall.

There's nothing exclusively "psalmish" about preaching in series. But series preaching of the psalms can be considered a genre-sensitive strategy for these reasons:

1. Intertextuality. Psalms by the same author, type, or liturgical setting, and psalms with shared themes, metaphors, and symbols can be read in light of one another.
2. Evidence of editorial arrangement. As noted above, the Psalter is not a randomly-arranged anthology, but a purposefully edited book. It may be too long a book to preach from beginning to end without a break, but shorter series will enable the

---

12 *War Psalms of the Prince of Peace* is the title of a book by James E. Adams (Presbyterian & Reformed, 1991).

congregation to hear it as a work of literature and not an assortment of stand-alone pieces.

3. The Psalter is obviously and self-consciously a book of corporate worship. Those who penned, edited, and collected the psalms clearly expected them to be used by God's people gathered in his presence. To preach them is to say, "Let's take a closer look at these songs we sing and these prayers we pray. What is God saying to us in these words we say to him?"

For Further Study

Allen, Ronald B. *And I Will Praise Him: A Guide to Worship in the Psalms.* Kregel, 1992.

Witvliet, John D. *The Biblical Psalms in Christian Worship.* Eerdmans, 2007.

Van Harn, Roger E., and Brent A. Strawn, eds. *Psalms for Preaching and Worship.* Eerdmans, 2009. (Subtitled "A Lectionary Commentary," this volume offers brief exegetical essays on 103 psalms as well as reflections on how to use psalms in ways other than preaching. A closing section includes much of the material in John Witvliet's *The Biblical Psalms in Christian Worship.*)

Crown and Covenant Publications: https://www.crownandcovenant.com for metrical Psalters, family worship resources and more.

Sons of Korah, Australian band that performs the Psalms. https://sonsofkorah.com

Wilson, Gerald H. "The Structure of the Psalter." Pages 229–246 in *Interpreting the Psalms.* Edited by David Firth and Philip S. Johnston. IVP, 1990.

Talk about It

Choose a psalm you've preached or plan to preach. See if you and your fellow students or fellow pastors can think of at least three ways you could use this psalm elsewhere in the service.

Dig Deeper

Survey the resources on musical and dramatic renderings of psalms in John D. Witvliet, *The Biblical Psalms in Christian Worship*, pages 92–127. Use one or more in an upcoming worship service where a psalm is the sermon text.

Practice

1. Write a one-sentence introduction to a psalm you might ask someone to use before reading the text in a worship service.
2. Survey musical and metrical versions of your psalm text; select one that best fits your congregation and teach it to them before or after preaching the psalm.
3. Use a video clip by *The Sons of Korah* as an offertory or prelude. https://sonsofkorah.com

Conclusion

Genre-sensitive strategies like those sketched in these pages aim to help preachers honor the poemness of psalms and to help congregations experience the affective, imaginative, and aesthetic dimensions of biblical poems in ways that traditional approaches to preaching might not permit. My operating assumption, shaped by studying homiletics and biblical poetry, but more importantly, by my own painful experience in trying to preach the psalms, is well stated by Thomas Long:

> Preachers who have sought to be open and attentive to biblical texts in their preaching have long sensed that a sermon on a psalm, for example, ought somehow to be different from one that grows out of a miracle story, not only because of *what* the two texts say but also because of *how* the texts say what they say. A psalm is poetry, a miracle story is narrative; and because they are two distinct literary and rhetorical forms, they "come at" the reader in different ways and create contrasting effects. What is needed, then, is a process of sermon development sufficiently nuanced to recognize and employ these differences in the creation of the sermon itself.[1]

Other genre-sensitive strategies could be suggested. Not every strategy will fit equally well with every psalm. Some should be used sparingly (I would not want to preach in the mode of explication

---

1 Thomas G. Long, *Preaching and the Literary Forms of the Bible* (Fortress, 1989), 11.

very often, for example). The strategies are not mutually exclusive: we need not choose between preaching an image and preaching an emotion. We might re-narratize a psalm and pay attention to words; read the psalm well and surround the sermon with other elements of worship that maximize the congregation's experience of the poem. Sometimes preachers will succeed and fail at genre-sensitivity in the same sermon. I recently read a sermon that imposed a contrived alliterated outline on a Psalm (contrary to my strategy #3), but its vocabulary (strategy #8) and word pictures (strategy #2) were far more poetic than average. The sermon succeeded.

In one way or another, preachers who wish to honor the Bible that God actually gave us—not a compendium of theological propositions, but rich, varied literature—will have to shape sermons on psalms so as to engage emotion, imagination, and aesthetics. All too often, these poetic concerns are lost in preaching the psalms because, as Fred Craddock put it, ". . . the minister boils off all the water and then preaches the stain in the bottom of the cup."[2]

I hope this book helps ministers who do not want to give up preaching the psalms, but are not content with preaching the psalmy stain in the cup either.

---

2 Fred Craddock, *Preaching* (Abingdon, 1985), 123.

Appendix 1

Preach All the Psalms,
Preach Whole Psalms

Two questions remain regarding the suitability of psalms as sermon texts: first, should we preach all the psalms, or are there, perhaps, some which are unsuitable for the pulpit? And second, should we ever preach just a portion (a stanza, a verse or two, or maybe just a line) of a psalm, or only the entire poem? Neither question can be treated here at length.

Preach all the Psalms?

There have probably been those in every age who would agree with John Wesley that some psalms are "unfit for the mouths of the Christian congregation."[1] Presumably, if Wesley balked at praying or singing these unfit psalms, he'd not want to preach on them either. What he balked at, of course, were the imprecatory psalms, in which the poets curse or asks God to curse their enemies.[2] Any sensitive Christian has wondered whether we who follow Jesus

---

1 "It is surely legitimate to question whether the whole Psalter should be included in Christian worship ... or whether the Psalter should be censored at those points which seem to be inconsistent with God's revelation in Jesus Christ." Bernhard W. Anderson, *Out of the Depths* (Westminster, 1983), 88. Anderson goes on to cite Christoph Barth and Dietrich Bonhoeffer in support of using all the Psalms.

2 Sometimes "imprecatory psalms" are listed as a class. One problem with this is the overlap between this designation and other generic categories into which the same psalms fit. Another problem is the subjective call: how much imprecation must a psalm contain before it is considered an imprecatory Psalm? Imprecations appear in many psalms. For a good index of these, see Appendix 3 in James E. Adams, *War Psalms of the Prince of Peace* (Presbyterian & Reformed,

should endorse and use these cursing psalms. Fortunately, despite our misgivings about some of this disturbing psalmic language, interpreters of various theological stripes have defended their use as legitimate expression.[3] Dietrich Bonhoeffer thought, "We ought not to select psalms at our own discretion, thinking that we know better what we ought to pray than does God himself."[4] What he says of praying psalms is true of preaching psalms. All of them may be regarded as part of God's Word to his people and therefore preachable.

Some of the individual psalms of lament do not curse anyone, but can still be a challenge to preach because they mention enemies, and unlike the Hebrew poets, we do not have any literal enemies.[5] Everybody in our congregation has to endure difficulties of various kinds, but hardly anyone we know personally is under threat of death. A preacher might try to make these texts relevant to the ordinary problems of everyday life, trivializing them in the process, so that the "enemy" of the psalm is identified with depression or unemployment or a sour marriage. Some in the congregation may be predisposed to hear this kind of application. One woman I knew used to regularly ask for prayer for help in dealing with an "enemy," her landlord. Over time, it became clear why she

---

1991), or the lecture "Preaching Imprecatory Psalms" by John Mark Hicks on his web site, johnmarkhicks.faithsite.com.

3 Help in handling the imprecatory psalms can be found in Allender and Longman, *The Cry of the Soul: How Our Emotions Reveal Our Deepest Questions About God* (NavPress, 1994), 65–78; Bernhard Anderson, *Out of the Depths* (Westminster, 1983), 82–93; J. Clinton McCann, *A Theological Introduction to the Book of Psalms* (Abingdon, 1993), 112–124; Eugene H. Peterson, *Answering God* (HarperCollins, 1989), 95–103; Adams, *War Psalms*; and James L. Mays, *Preaching and Teaching the Psalms* (Westminster John Knox), 14–16. These authors do not all take the same approach, but they have this in common: none of them dismisses the cursing psalms from consideration by Christian preachers.

4 Dietrich Bonhoeffer, *Psalms: The Prayer Book of the Bible,* trans. James H. Burtness (Augsburg, 1970), 26

5 J. Clinton McCann, who worked closely on the Psalms for many years before visiting Latin America, testifies that not until he sat with Guatemalan believers whose lives and liberties were threatened by powerful warlords did he grasp what it must have felt like for the psalmists to write about enemies. "Greed, Grace, and Gratitude," in *Performing the Psalms*, ed. Dave Bland and David Fleer (Chalice, 2005), 53–54.

regarded him as an enemy: he wanted his rent on time and insisted she honor the lease she signed stipulating no pets. I did sympathize with this woman, an individual as broken and needy as I've ever met. But to have given her the justification or assurance she craved by equating her situation with that of the psalmists would have been ludicrous.

Likewise, many of the corporate laments may be difficult for a North American pastor to preach, as our congregations are situated so differently from the Israelites who first prayed these agonized prayers. Too many sermons have trivialized the laments by spiritualizing the enemies or putting minor troubles (conflict with local authorities over a building permit, stagnant giving, and the like) in the same category as impending national disaster. A preacher who cannot yet see how a given psalm of lament applies to his congregation would be well-advised to save that text for another day or, perhaps, preach it as a call to prayerful solidarity with brothers and sisters in other parts of the world where enemies are a very real threat.[6]

It is not only the cursing psalms or some of the more pointed laments that pose a challenge for preachers. What homiletical use is to be made of Psalm 45, "A Wedding Song," for example? Unless it is allegorized, it's hard to see how the poem will preach.[7]

But the challenge of discovering theologically faithful contemporary relevance is hardly unique to the Psalter. Texts that are hard to preach can be found in every book of the Bible. Preachers should be slow to conclude that any Scripture text *cannot* yield an exegetically, theologically faithful sermon.

Preach Whole Psalms?

A library search of collected sermons on the psalms reveals that preaching psalm portions is far more common than preaching

6 John Mark Hicks offers some helpful suggestions on preaching communal laments in chapter 4 of Bland and Fleer, *Performing the Psalms*.

7 The argument could be made that the use of this psalm in Hebrews 1:8–9 legitimizes allegorization. John Goldingay (following Spurgeon) spiritualizes it somewhat in *Songs from a Strange Land* (InterVarsity, 1978), 93.

whole psalms.[8] Of the five hundred sermons indexed in *Twenty Centuries of Great Preaching,*[9] only sixteen cite psalm texts. Of these, only two purport to exposit an entire psalm, and only one of these actually does so. Not one of John Donne's thirty-four extant sermons on psalms or Spurgeon's *Sermons on the Psalms* or Clovis Chappell's *Sermons from the Psalms* treats an entire psalm. Most exposit a single verse.[10]

But despite this long (and noble?) tradition of preaching psalm portions, there are compelling arguments for preaching whole psalms. Psalms, like all poems, are literary units. Something is lost when a line is extracted from its context.

What's lost may be an accurate sense of the quoted portion. For example, Reinhold Niebuhr took Psalm 2:4, "The One enthroned in heaven laughs," as the text for a sermon on "Humor and Faith."[11] But there's nothing humorous about the laughter in Psalm 2! This laughter voices God's withering scorn for his enemies. Psalms are so full of striking, memorable lines, preachers may be tempted to make "points" out of them quite foreign to their meaning in context.

What's lost by not preaching entire psalms may be balance. Laments, if preached without their confident turn to praise, will leave hearers with only half a story and no gospel. On the other hand, preaching only a psalm's expression of confidence because we would rather not deal with the shocking honesty of lament will not be true to the poem or to life, as any congregant with her Bible open to the text will see at a glance.

---

8 Notable exceptions include James Boice's three volume expository commentary, *Psalms* (Baker, 1994, 1996, 1998); John Goldingay, *Songs from a Strange Land*; Eugene Peterson, *A Long Obedience in the Same Direction* (InterVarsity, 1980), and *Where Your Treasure Is* (Eerdmans, 1993).

9 Clyde E. Fant and William M. Pinson, compilers (Word, 1971).

10 Charles Haddon Spurgeon, *C. H. Spurgeon's Sermons on the Psalms* (Zondervan, 1960); Clovis G. Chappell, *Sermons from the Psalms* (Abingdon, 1931). Brigham Young University has an on line searchable, printable collection of John Donne's sermons: http://www.lib.byu.edu/donne.

11 In Reinhold Niebuhr, *Discerning the Signs of the Times* (Charles Scribner's Sons, 1946), 111–131.

What's lost may be the intended mood or tone of the quoted psalm portion. A preacher announces Psalm 90:12 as his text: "Teach us to number our days aright, that we may gain a heart of wisdom." The sermon will make the same *general* claim as this oft-quoted verse: we ought to take life's brevity into account in the way we live. But how? "Gather ye rosebuds while ye may"? "You only go around once in life, so ya' gotta grab for all the gusto you can"? The preacher who intends to develop a sermon along these lines had better find another text! Psalm 90:12, in the context of the entire poem, sobers us with the indignation and wrath of a holy God.

Good preaching does not pluck verses out of context; certainly this is true of good preaching of the psalms. If only a psalm portion is to be preached, the expositor must be sure that it is not distorted due to ignoring the poem's informing imagery, allusions, mood, or tone. Ordinarily it is best to preach whole psalms.

Appendix 2

Sample Sermons

"Trust"
Psalm 131
Thomas H Troeger[1]

Four lanes of traffic at sixty miles an hour. Tractor-trailers, family wagons, VW bugs, sports cars, pickup trucks and our Greyhound bus were all driving as though the highway behind them was being rolled up like a carpet to be taken to the cleaners. If we didn't get out of the way fast enough, we would be rolled up with it.

Across the aisle in the bus a baby was sleeping. The mother had spread a diaper over her left shoulder and held the child there as though he were no burden at all.

The diesel's hum. The squealing brakes. Honking horns. The roar of rubber buffing concrete. Suicidal drivers who crossed without signaling from the far left-hand lane to exits on the right. None of these disturbed the child. He slept through it all.

Prayer is trusting God the way that child trusted his mother:

But I have calmed and quieted my soul,
    like a child quieted at its mother's breast;
    like a child that is quieted is my soul.
(Psalm 131:2)

It is a lovely verse and fills us with warmth. But how does it become

---

1 This sermon is chapter ten in *Rage, Reflect, Rejoice*, by Thomas Troeger (Westminster, 1977). Used by permission of the publisher.

real for us? We are no longer babies. We are in the driver's seat
now, and if we took our eyes off the road for one second, we would
get clobbered by the fool who is tailgating or the moving van that
wants to squeeze between us and the orange Camaro.

Life crowds us. We drive through it with the rest of the world at
breakneck speed. We need to pull over and stop.

Prayer involves deliberately setting aside time to get out of life's
heavy traffic. This takes discipline. We keep thinking we'll drive
just a little farther through the day's routine. We'll make one more
phone call. We will dictate one more letter. We will get just this last
thing done. Then we will take a break. But we do not. We keep
driving on.

Certain types of prayer demand that we stop, that we make a
conscious effort to still our revved up motors. This kind of prayer
is not instigated by experiences that dramatically confront us with
God's presence. Neither a close call nor a thunderstorm is the occasion for the psalmist's irenic state. His profoundly peaceful prayer
does not even depend on a theological theme or a rich spiritual insight or reflection on the mysteries of God. Quite to the contrary.
The psalmist has disengaged himself from any exalted vision or
probing thought:

> O Lord, my heart is not lifted up,
>   my eyes are not raised too high:
> I do not occupy myself with things
>   too great and too marvelous for me.
> (Psalm 131:1)

Prayer is not always strenuous. It does not always take us to the
gate of heaven or lead us through shaking experiences of rebirth
and wonder.

Prayer is leaning on God as a child leans on the mother's breast.
This is not just a sentimental image. The psalmist describes a process that leads to the awareness of God's parental care.

"My heart is not lifted up." The psalmist sets aside his emotions.
He does not seek the fervent experience of God's Spirit burning or
thundering inside him. He does not request that God change his

life or take away his sin or make him a new creation. There will be other times when the psalmist can deal with these desires. Then his heart will throb from wrestling with God. For now the psalmist's heart beats with the quiet pulse of one whose sleep is dreamless and secure.

Prayer is being in God's presence and knowing that we do not have to share everything we feel. As a genuine friend and a loving parent, God is glad simply to be with us. We feel the comfort of being understood without being exposed.

"My eyes are not raised too high." The psalmist does not let visual reality stun him with beauty or grandeur. He does not seek an inspiring vision. He does not become involved with his environment, but relaxes his sight.

Prayer is taking time out from our surroundings. It is reducing the visual assault of the world. It is like traveling from a tourist trap filled with the neon lights to a park area where there are no signs or billboards. The visual difference can actually be sensed inside us. We do not feel so badgered and crowded by the demands of others.

Prayer is turning our three-way lamp down to 60 watts and laying aside the newspaper and being satisfied with the softer light and God's presence in the silence of the moment.

Our dimmer physical vision represents a less intense interior gaze. We do not squint the eyes of the soul, but relax and enjoy whatever gentle light shines within.

"I do not occupy myself with things too great and too marvelous for me." Prayer is not always deep. It is not always involved with the most perplexing or the most anguished questions of existence. Prayer does not always give its attention to the Bible and how God has acted in history for the salvation of humanity. Prayer can lay off the heavy stuff.

Prayer is letting the mind wander freely in the presence of God. No great revelations. No great struggles. Simple reflections that meander into fantasies and evaporate into reveries.

Prayer is the sense of unembarrassed security that we have as we doze in our favorite easy chair. Prayer is day dreaming on God's shoulder. If we cannot relax this much around God, then we have yet to perceive just how loving God is.

The mother on the bus knew that her child needed to sleep. She meanwhile kept reading and got up twice to let the passenger next to the window in and out of his seat. All the time the child rested soundly on her shoulder.

God is like that mother. God does not demand that we always give close attention to the world or to God's greatness. God knows that we need someone against whom we can lean and sleep.

Prayer is being a child in the presence of our divine parent. Just as the baby on the bus knew that the mother would not drop him, so we know that God will never drop us.

Prayer is discovering the truth of Jesus' statement that "whoever does not receive the kingdom of God like a child shall not enter it" (Mark 10:15). When we trust God "like a child quieted at its mother's breast," then we enter the kingdom. Peace. Security. Utterly dependable love. These are all ours. Not as statements of belief subject to doubt, but as the very truth of life. We rest on God with the same unquestioning trust that the child had in his mother.

The child did not feel self-conscious or awkward. He trusted because that was all he could do. There was no other option. Faith and life were of one piece for the child.

Prayer leads us to see that there is no other option for us than to trust in God. In prayer we find God to be one absolute security of our life. We decide to put God above the aspirations of our heart, the visions of our soul, and the thoughts of our mind. We trust God more than any of these internal subjective processes, and in that act of uncalculated and unconditional trust we find serenity.

> O Israel, hope in the Lord from this time forth and for
>   evermore.
> (Psalm 131:3)

The psalmist's final verse snaps us out of our restful mood. One minute the psalmist is talking about a quiet scene between mother and child, and the next he is ending his prayer with an exhortation to Israel. How can we account for the abrupt change other than understanding it as an instruction to the congregation? What inner dynamic leads from the gentle picture of maternal love to the national state?

Security. The psalmist has discovered a bedrock security in his relationship with God that makes all other claims to security seem weak and fraudulent. The trust in military power. The protection of Jerusalem's walls. The alliances with foreign powers. The national economy. All the resources that the state claims will keep us secure are seen as the undependable human contrivances which in fact they are.

Prayer does not deny the necessity of political attempts to establish the security of society. But prayer reveals the tenuous nature of every human arrangement. Prayer is discovering the flimsiness of society and the durability of God.

Hoping in the Lord is not icing to cover the cake of power politics. Hoping in the Lord is the prerequisite of sane national government. If the people of Israel first trust God "like a child quieted at its mother's breast," then they can be objective about the nation's attempts at security. They will not look to the state to provide their fundamental security as persons, since God already furnishes that. They will not deify the nation, nor expect any political organization to fulfill their basic needs for an enduring source of comfort and strength.

Prayer is seeing through the propaganda of politics. Daydreaming on God's shoulder is an act that steals the thunder from the exaggerated promises of politicians and the extraordinary claims of the state. When we "hope in the Lord from this time forth and for evermore," we look at our nation realistically. Our compromises, our alliances, our policies issue from the calm soul of a people whose most basic faith is in God. We may fail. Our nation may totter, but we will not panic, because we know that the arms which hold us will never let us go.

Children who have not been raised by dependable and loving people frequently spend much of their adult life searching for the security they lacked when young. They missed the experience of the baby on the bus who felt safe on his mother's shoulder.

The distortion of power politics may represent at a national level the same search for security that marks an individual's life. Just as the individual has not known the comfort of dependable parents, so the nation has not known the strength of God. The nation then turns exclusively to military and economic strategies, while neglecting those qualities without which a society becomes rotten at its core: integrity, justice, God's moral law.

Prayer is discovering the political significance of trusting God. Prayer frees people from the bondage of national pride by bringing them into the presence of life's only ultimate security. When a nation's people have been "calmed and quieted" by God's strength, then they know the wisdom of the psalmist's instruction, "hope in the Lord from this time forth and for evermore."

"Desiring God"
Psalm 84
Ken Langley

Camp Sankanac is a holy place. You will not find it on the maps in the back of your Bible. It's located on the French Creek in eastern Pennsylvania. It's where I grew up going to summer camp, where as a teenager, I joined the staff, where I made a lot of memories. I still remember, though it's been years, the smell of the pine trees. I remember the roughhewn planks that we sat on for camp fires. I remember feeling the front of me bake while the back of me froze. I can remember the buzz of the mosquitoes and the sound of the sap popping in the camp fire, the sound of the guitar strumming, and the sound of young voices raised in praise to God. I met God there.

Do you have a place where you remember meeting God? Maybe a trail you hike, or a path you walk while you pray in the morning, or a favorite chair where you open God's word. Maybe this sanctuary. Someplace where you meet God.

For the poet who wrote Psalm 84, that place was the sanctuary in Jerusalem. He didn't get to go there as often as he liked, and when he did go, he didn't get to stay as long he wished. But memories of that holy place filled him with longing. Longing is written all over this poem—longing for the fair beauty of the Lord.

How lovely is your dwelling place, O Lord Almighty!

How lovely. There's beauty in God and the places where we meet God. There's something aesthetically satisfying about experiencing God. Or at least there *should* be. There are a lot of folks for whom religion is all ethics and no aesthetics, all duty and no beauty. And it's no wonder that those who meet them are turned off to the Christian message. It's not so much that they've been reasoned or argued out of it, it's just that they don't find it attractive.

There are others, and this psalmist is one, who believe not only because they have sufficient reason to believe, and not only obey because they sense the rightness of God's claim on their lives, but because they've been drawn to the beauty of God and the beauty of worship.

The psalmists celebrate the beauty of the Lord because life is experienced not only in terms of true and false, right and wrong, good and bad. Life is also experienced as beautiful and ugly. So these poets are repelled by evil and drawn to the moral beauty of God, and invite us to share this experience. They're caught up, not only in the rightness of God and the justice of God and the truth of God; they're enraptured by the beauty of God. Isn't he beautiful? Beautiful, isn't he?

Isn't he? Verse two.

> My soul yearns, even faints, for the courts of the Lord;
>   my heart and my flesh cry out for the living God.

One verb will not do, so he piles up successively stronger words for desire. "Yearn" is strong in both Hebrew and English, but not strong enough. So he says, "I faint!" This is the experience of a hiker in the arid stretches of the Grand Canyon, or a soldier who's marched twenty miles with a heavy pack and can't wait to flop down on the ground, drink some water, and close his eyes. The psalmist is light-headed with desire for the courts of the Lord, the place where he meets God.

His soul hungers for God with a pain that's almost physical, an intense desire for the living God – so we see that what matters is not so much the place where we meet God but God himself. Any place can be a sacred space if God is there, and any room can be a sanctuary if we meet God there. And he desires this intensely.

In fact, as he imagines Jerusalem and getting back to the place where he has met God, he remembers (perhaps from the last time he made the pilgrimage?) seeing some birds who had built their nests on the temple site, and he thinks to himself, "Lucky birds!" Verse three:

> Even the sparrow has found a home, and the swallow a nest
>   for herself,
>   where she may have her young—
> a place near your altar,
>   O Lord Almighty, my King and my God.

This is the language of love poetry. This is the kind of imagery you expect to find in sonnets and other lyrics that express strong emotion. "Why do birds suddenly appear every time you are near? Just like me, they long to be close to you." (Karen Carpenter, "Close to You.") This is the way the poet feels about God. "If only I could live near God like those birds who have their nests right there, at the temple."

> "Blessed are those who dwell in your house. They are ever praising you" (v. 4).

About fifteen years ago I visited Camp Sankanac, having not been there for a long, long time. I wanted my kids to see this place that featured so prominently in many of the bedtime stories I'd told them over the years. So we walked around for a couple of hours, seeing familiar sites and a number of changes. I saw teenagers and college students who were there working on staff for the summer and I thought, "Oh, how lucky you are! And you do not even know it—how fortunate you are to be in this special place for the whole summer!"

I think that's how the poet felt about the priests and Levites and temple servants and singers and maybe even the custodians who lived on the temple precincts. How wonderful it must be to live there and be ever praising the Lord.

Now and then somebody will say something like this to me, "How wonderful it must be to be a pastor; to work at the church, and to spend all your time in the Bible and in the things of God. And it is a wonderful privilege, though reality is seldom the same as fantasy. The pastorate, like any profession, has its mundane aspects and its days that are, you know, not all that great. And so, perhaps, the people who did live at the temple didn't experience one mountaintop experience after another as the psalmist fantasizes, but we'll let his imagination run because this is poetry, after all.

"Oh, how blessed," he thinks, "How happy, how lucky, how fortunate and to be envied are those who are in God's presence all the time because, in his presence, hurts are healed and in his presence, burdens are lifted, and in his presence, problems shrink as we get wrapped up in a God who is bigger than our problems. And in his presence (some of us have experienced this in corporate worship) we want to say, "Yes! This is what I was made for!"

But life is not one long unbroken experience of sensing God's presence. Life is not always the mountaintop, sometimes it's the valley. And so I'm glad that the psalmist goes on to write a second stanza in his poem about desiring God. I'm going to read verse five, but first let me repeat verse four, the end of the first stanza,

> Blessed are those who dwell in your house; they are ever praising you.
> But blessed too are those whose strength is in you, who have set their hearts on pilgrimage.
> As they pass through the Valley of Baca, they make it a place of springs; the autumn rains also cover it with pools.
> They go from strength to strength, till each appears before God in Zion.

Blessed are those who already have arrived in Zion, those who live there, those who are always in the presence of God. But blessed, too, are those who are on the way. Blessed are those who are where they want to be—with him. Blessed, too, are those who are on pilgrimage—not there yet but trying to get there. Blessed are those who get to spend their summers at Camp Sankanac. Blessed too are those who have to get up every day and have to go to work in Lake County or Kenosha. Blessed are those birds—the sparrows and the swallows who built their nests on the temple courts. Blessed, too, are we geese who are still migrating south. Blessed are those *on the road toward God*. Thank God for the second stanza of this poem. There's a blessing for us who are still on the way.

The valley of Baca is aptly named. It's not only an arid place but the word, "baca," in Hebrew sounds like the word for "weeping," so that the poet, (and poets do delight in deliberate ambiguity) probably wants us to think not of either dryness or weeping but both. The experience of pilgrimage is often an experience of spiritual dryness and/or sorrow. You'll find a contemporary translation of the Bible that renders this expression "the valley of the weepers," and you'll find another one that calls it "the arid valley." It's both/and.

Certainly, the Christian experience is sometimes an experience of weeping, or why would half of the psalms be laments? Half of them are songs of sorrow, complaint, weeping. Why would Jesus, the Incarnate God, be called, "the Man of Sorrows" if weeping was not a big part of life? In the last generation, a man writing advice to preachers said, "There's a broken heart in every pew. Preach to the sorrowing and you will never lack for a congregation." It's part of life, part of life before God.

And so is dryness, spiritual dryness. It's part of our experience if for no other reason than because we are animals as well as souls. Our physical bodies are not capable of sustaining the constant spiritual high that we might desire. We might like to live up there on the heights all the time, but we all know, do we not, that our bodies and other parts of our personality cause us to have this up and down kind of experience, so there is dryness. Sometimes life is like Camp Sankanac; sometimes it's the Valley of Baca.

But notice that those on pilgrimage, whom the psalmist pronounces blessed, make that valley a place of springs. They dig wells where others only see dust. As they move toward the fuller experience of God's presence that they long for, they find ways to create oases along the way. Do you know anyone like this? People who've learned to see disappointments as divine appointments, people who've discovered that pain is sometimes the tool of the divine surgeon, folks who see problems as opportunities for God to work, people who can sing, and really mean it:

I thank God for the mountains and I thank him for the valleys.
I thank him for the storms he's brought me through.
For if I never had a problem, I wouldn't know that he could solve them.
I wouldn't know what faith in God could do.

I'm not talking here about a rose-colored-glasses outlook on life, a Pollyannaish point of view. This is not the "if life hands you a lemon, make lemonade" philosophy. If that's your personality, if you're an optimistic person, great; life will be a whole lot cheerier for you. But I'm talking about a God-thing here, a gift of God's grace to those who, whatever their personality type, find the strength that he alone provides to dig wells and make springs in dry places.

It's not just human effort that replaces dryness with refreshment. It's God, and God alone, who can send the needed rains. *"The autumn rains cover it with pools,"* the end of verse six. It's a dry valley but the autumn rains make it a place of pools.

The Jews celebrated the New Year at the end of September, occasioning pilgrimages like the one this psalmist is on or remembering. After the long, hot summer, autumn rains were a welcome relief and were viewed as a gracious gift from the hand of God.

That's how God treats his children still. If you're on pilgrimage this morning, remembering but not experiencing at present a refreshing sense of God's presence, this verse assures you that droughts do not last forever. It may seem that you've been dry for a long, long time, but the autumn rains will come. They always do. God does not neglect those who thirst for him. Sometimes we experience God, sometimes we just desire God, sometimes we only desire to desire God. Wherever you're at this morning, this portrait of pilgrimage encourages you to just keep on truckin'. Keep going. Put one foot in front of another. Do not give up—you'll get there. God will provide some cool, refreshing places along the way. He will not forget you.

This portrait begins and ends with strength. Verse five: *Blessed are those whose strength is in you."* Verse seven: *"They go from strength to strength."* Strength sufficient for this day, this hour, maybe for this minute. God strengthens them to keep going.

Verses eight and nine seem like a parenthesis. My guess is that as the poet was on his way to Jerusalem, whether literally or in his imagination, he was prompted to include in his prayers the king who lived there. That's who the shield is in verse nine, the symbol of strength or sovereignty. "Lord, I do not only pray for myself, I pray for our leaders, I pray for the king." And then, verse ten, third stanza of the poem, he's back to his main point . . .

> Better is one day in your courts than a thousand elsewhere;
> I would rather be a doorkeeper in the house of my God
> than dwell in the tents of the wicked.

Two images here—one temporal, one spatial. The temporal image: one day with God is better than a thousand without him. The spatial image: I'd rather stand outside the gate then sit comfortably in the house, if God is outside and the ungodly are inside. I hope you believe that. I hope that expresses not just the poet's view but your own as well, like it did for one professor who talked to J. I. Packer. Some of you who've read *Knowing God* may remember this incident. Packer is talking with an older gentleman, an outspoken Christian whose Christianity had cost him in academia. The powers-that-be in his university did not appreciate someone as vocal as he was about his faith in Christ, so it had cost him promotions and respect. And as the two of them were talking about some of the costs of Christian commitment, the older man said, "None of that matters, for I have known God, and they haven't."

Better one day with God than a thousand elsewhere, better to be a humble doorkeeper than to be inside with the godless. This morning we sang, "I'd rather have Jesus than anything this world affords today." It's easier to sing those words than to truly mean them. As Mother Theresa used to put it, "You'd better not say 'Jesus is all I need' unless Jesus is all you've got." Well, God grant us the grace I believe he granted this psalmist to sing and to mean words like these: "Bring me back to you," and "It is you we adore," and "I'm desperate for you," and "The greatest thing in all the world is knowing you," and "Lord, I want to be where you are dwelling daily in your presence."

Why? Why desire God that intensely? Up till now, the poet has described his desire, but he hasn't really *explained* it. He hasn't said *why* God is so beautiful, *why* God's presence is so desirable. He does that now at the end of the poem. Verse eleven:

> For the LORD God is a sun and shield;
> the LORD bestows favor and honor;

no good thing does he withhold from those whose walk is
blameless.

Once again, there are two images of what makes God so eminent-
ly desirable. As sun, he's the source of warmth and blessing and
life and everything that we enjoy on this planet that relies on the
sun. As shield – this time Shield with a capital "S," not the king
referred to in verse nine, but the king "par excellence" – as Shield,
he protects us from anything bad that comes our way. He gives us
all good things, he protects us from all bad things. *"No good thing
does he withhold."*

Do you believe that? *"No good thing does he withhold."* There
may be things that you think would be good for you, and you do
not have them. But if it was really good for you to have it – now –
God would give it to you. Because *"no good thing does he withhold
from those whose walk is blameless."*

Sometimes, Christians have this notion that if we desire to get
anything out of our relationship to God, we have somehow poi-
soned it, that we ought to somehow be disinterested and just live
the Christian life because it's right to do so, and worship because
God deserves it. But as soon as we start to think, "Maybe there's
something in it for me," then we've spoiled it.

That's not the way the Bible looks at things. From cover to cover, the Bible unembarrassedly promises reward. God is a rewarder
of those who diligently seek him. He offers to fill our cup. He does
not need anything from us. We, on the other hand, are needy and
the most God-honoring thing we can do is say, "God, fill me. Bless
me. Enrich me out of your overflowing supply."

At a church in a city that had a university and divinity school,
there was a professor from the seminary who served as an usher
in the balcony of his church. One day, the pastor said something
to him, "You know, you've got two earned doctorates. Your books
are read and respected everywhere. And yet, you serve the Lord in
this humble way here. You ought to be, it seems to me, more prominently featured instead of tucked away in the balcony just helping
people find their seats and handing them bulletins." The professor
quoted verse ten of our text, *"I'd rather be a doorkeeper in the house*

of my God." What a great honor to stand by the door in the place where people meet God! What more could anybody ask for?

"O Lord Almighty," verse twelve, "blessed is the man who trusts in you." I was surprised to learn that Psalm 84 is the only one in the collection that uses this word "blessed" three times. That's surprising to me because "blessed" is a common word in the psalms, a common word in the Bible, and yet, this medium-length psalm is the only one to use it as many as three times.

The poet uses it to mark the moods of his poem. The first "blessed" in verse four is wistful. "Oh, lucky birds! Blessed are those who get to live at the temple all the time, for they are ever praising God." The "blessed" in verse five is resolute: "But blessed, too, are we who aren't there yet, but are determined to get there. We're on pilgrimage, and we're headed toward God."

And then, lastly, the "blessed" in verse 12: blessed are all, wherever you find yourself today, who are satisfied in God., who desire God, who at least desire to desire, or desire to desire to desire God! If you're in there somewhere, you're blessed! You're blessed, this poem says, if right now your heart is so filled with joy in the presence of God that you're going to leave church saying, "Yes! I cannot wait 'til next week!" But you're also blessed if you're more like the Englishman who wrote in his diary, "Went to church today. Was not too greatly disappointed."

Let's pray.

"Wait for the Morning"
Psalm 130
Ken Langley

A few months ago, right after the Virginia Tech University massacre, the worship leader at a community worship service turned to this text. On behalf of those gathered to find solace in God in the wake of that awful tragedy, he stood and prayed the first two verses of this Psalm, "Out of the depths we cry to you, O Lord. O Lord, hear our voice. Let your ears be attentive to our cry for mercy."

I'm not surprised that these words were selected for that occasion. Down through the centuries, God's people have often made these words their own when going through deep grief.

Like other psalmists, our poet images trouble as being in the depths. Sometimes in the psalms the depths are a pit, sometimes mire, sometimes deep water – whatever the specifics, the imagery conveys feelings of helplessness in the face of heart-breaking bereavement, victimization, or, as in the case of the Virginia Tech shootings, senseless tragedy. No light and momentary troubles here; people are in the *depths,* and out of the depths they cry, "O Lord, hear my voice." They beg, "Let your ears be attentive to our cry for mercy."

So I say, I'm not surprised that these words might seem fitting for the Virginia Tech service. But there *is* a surprise in the next line of the poem. At least, *I* was surprised the first time I read this Psalm with care. "If you, O Lord, kept a record of sins, O Lord, who could stand?" What surprises me is that the depths this poet talks about are not depths of illness or oppression or violence or bereavement, but depths of guilt. Unlike most psalms where this imagery is used, here it's not a case of enemies digging a pit that he fell into, or the waves and breakers of life crashing over him and overwhelming him. No, he's in a hole he made himself; a pit of sin. And you and I make holes like that for ourselves like that all the time. This poet is one of us.

I heard about a man who never went to church except for weddings and funerals. With no religious background, he had no idea what happened in church, little notion of what was said, what people who go to church believe – though he assumed they viewed themselves as superior to irreligious people like him. A coworker persuaded him to try church at least once. So one Sunday morning he slipped in late so he wouldn't have to talk to anybody, arriving when the service was already in progress. He sat in the back pew just as the congregation was praying the corporate prayer of confession: "We have done which we ought not to have done and we have left undone that which we ought to have done." With something of a shock, he said to himself, "These are my kind of people!"

We're *all* his kind of people. All of us, believers included, find ourselves crying to God out of depths we're in because of our own sin.

I think of a guy who had an affair with his wife's sister. His wife forgave him. And he knew God forgave him. But he was still in the depths. His entire family was shamed, trust had to be rebuilt, he wondered how on earth they were going to put their lives back together.

I think of another man, also a Christian, who embezzled money from his company and was now doing jail time. He'd never broken a law in his life, had never been in trouble with the authorities, but he'd gotten himself in some financial difficulty and did something dumb. Now he's got a wife and children he won't see for at least three years. Even though he knows forgiveness, even though he knows that he's washed clean by the blood of Jesus—he's still in the depths of remorse.

These guys, like our poet, know grace, mercy, and forgiveness. But their emotional experience does not yet match their theology. They believe God is merciful, but they're not at the moment feeling the sunshine of his merciful smile on their lives. They know that God is kind, but they're still laid low.

The depths, are usually dark places: ocean deeps where blind fish swim, mines where light never comes unless technology brings it there. I know a canyon in Colorado so deep and so narrow the sun never shines on the canyon floor. Nothing grows there. The rock of the canyon bottom is cold, even in the mid-August. It's always dim twilight there.

Our poet is a believer, but he's still in that canyon. He knows that the sun is shining up there somewhere, but he cannot see it, cannot feel its warmth. He knows forgiveness but he's not *feeling* forgiven. He's still in the canyon, still in the depths.

And his experience is perfectly normal.

I didn't formerly think so. I used to think that only non-Christians had to pray, "out of the depths"; that believers, who know they're forgiven, ought to always *feel* forgiven – which to me meant, "feel just fine." But after fifty years of being a Christian, thirty of those years a pastor, and after reading John Owen's masterful exposition of Psalm 130 (*Forgiveness of Sin*), I believe that depths and darkness are normal for even the saintliest saint. That God sometimes permits his children to grieve and grieve deeply over sins that they know are forgiven. And though he washes them clean by the blood of his Son, he does not immediately lift the cloud that covers their hearts.

Why should this be? Why should God deal with his children this way? Why shouldn't it be that, once we know we're forgiven, we feel forgiven, and move on without pain, without any grief or sorrow over sin? Well, the answer is as varied as you and I. Like any good parent, God knows he has to treat us differently at different times and under different circumstances. But a general answer to that question—why does the darkness sometimes linger, why do we still find ourselves in the depths even though we know we're forgiven—is that God sometimes wants us to know the depth and darkness of sin. Not a theoretical knowledge, an *experiential* knowledge that we know not only with our head but with our heart.

Suppose you wound someone deeply. Not one of those casual hurts that happen every day, but really hurt somebody deeply. You get convicted about it. You confess. You claim 1 John 1:9: "If we confess our sins, he is faithful and just to forgive us our sins and to cleanse us from all unrighteousness." And immediately you think, "Well, that's taken care of; I feel pretty good now!"

What if the Spirit of God convicts you about a longstanding sin, some darkness that's gripped your heart for a long, long time? Maybe he helps you see yourself as he sees you, a bully who wounds people all the time, embittering them against you and against God.

You feel the darkness of this character flaw for a minute or two, maybe an hour or two, but then you confess, you come clean, and you think, "This conviction and confession business isn't so bad. Just get it over with and get on with life. No big deal."

If God did not sometimes let us experience longer seasons in the pits and in the dark, we might not take sin as seriously as he does.

The psalmist goes on to say in verse four, "With you there is forgiveness therefore, you are feared." You are feared. If we grasp what the poet grasped, we will not say, "Oh well, yes, I sinned, but thankfully, there's confession, and confession is not so bad. God likes to forgive." We'll say, "God, as bad as sin is, as deep and as dark as it is, I can hardly believe that you're willing to forgive. Your law tells me sin shouldn't be overlooked. My conscience tells me sin shouldn't be overlooked. And yet you forgive. I stand, I stand in awe of you, holy God to whom all praise is due."

When we come to the Lord's table and we're reminded of the terrible, terrible price that the Son of God had to pay that we might be forgiven, we cannot take sin lightly. We shudder, we cringe that it was our sins that bloodied his hands and feet, our transgressions that pierced his side. "Therefore, you are feared."

And then after we pray like that, we wait. "I wait for the Lord. My soul waits and in his word I put my hope." This word that tells me how God dealt with my sin, this word that promises forgiveness and eternity in a place where there is no more sin, where we will be beyond the reach of temptation, this book full of hope and promise, in this word I put my hope.

And I wait. I wait. Whoever wrote Psalm 119 says that his eyes were open through the watches of the night that he might mediate on God's promises – waiting, waiting through the night. Sometimes, in God's mercy we do not have to wait very long. The feeling of forgiveness follows hard on the heels of confession and we do not linger long in the depths.

But sometimes we wait, and we wait, and we wait. Sometimes we wait long because, although we've been forgiven, we keep on sinning. Eugene Peterson describes one sinner he knew (could have been you or me):

A few scabs dappled his white skin where he had scraped the bald spot on the top of his head. That's most of what I saw of him that day as he sat in my office. He kept his head down as he spoke, his eyes not willing to meet mine for more than a moment. I watched the way his knuckles bulged as he rubbed his hands together in anguish. I had lost count of the number of times I sat with him to hear his confession. It was more of the same this time—same old sins, same old failures—but it was different too. He was about to give up on trying to be a Christian. He wanted to know, 'Will not I ever get to the place in life where I will not have to ask God to forgive me for the things I do?' Heaven knows, I wanted to say, 'Yes, you will,' but I couldn't. I knew that he and I will never outgrow the need for the mercy and forgiveness of God. Not 'til the resurrection, that is. But for that we have to wait.

Other times we wait because God knows there are lessons we can learn only while waiting. He wants us to know our sin as he knows our sin. He wants us to feel about our sin what he feels about our sin.

Wait. "My soul waits for the Lord more than watchmen wait for the morning, more than watchmen wait for the morning." Verbatim repetition is rare in the psalms—these poets didn't waste many words. But here, the repetition is just right, evoking the kind of emotion we feel in Robert Frost's lines, "and miles to go before I sleep, and miles to go before I sleep." It's wistful, it's longing: "More than watchmen wait for the morning, more than watchmen wait for the morning."

It's hard to wait through the night. If you're a sentry on guard duty, if you're a night watchman who has to try and keep his eyes open in a lonely, quiet building, it's hard. I cannot stay awake all night; I just cannot do it. When we were young, Jennifer and I were sponsors for our church's youth group. We went with them on an all-nighter with one activity after another. Around 3 o'clock in the morning we went bowling, and as I sat waiting for my turn to bowl, I fell asleep. In Africa I attended an all-night worship service. Preaching and singing all night long (it was a little easier to stay awake during the singing than during the preaching). Late, late in the night I started to long for the dawn. I'd look at the horizon, willing the sun to rise: "Please, please, come up!" It's hard to stay awake all night long.

But you know something about this perfectly chosen image of the psalmist's? However long the night seems, the morning will surely come! It always comes, every day without fail. And however long those night hours, however long it might seem before God answers your prayer and lifts you out of the depths and into the sunlight once again, morning *will* come. Another psalmist says, "Weeping may last for the night, but joy comes in the morning." It does come. It *will* happen. Trust it. Trust him. God does not ignore or neglect his children who wait for him and hope in him. The morning will come.

Maybe it will come for you today when we meet at the Lord's table and take those communion elements to our lips, and you're reminded that the steadfast love of the Lord never changes. Maybe deep will call to deep – depths of mercy answering depths of sorrow over sin – and the sunshine will break through for you again. Maybe dawn will break when your season of darkness has sufficiently humbled you, broken you, and made you sense the depth and darkness of your sin. But this I promise: the darkness will not last, for any child of God, one hour longer than the Father knows best. Then—morning!

Confident of this, the psalmist ends his poem: "O Israel! Put your hope in the Lord, for with the Lord is unfailing love and with him is full redemption. He himself will redeem Israel from all their sins. " Put your hope in the Lord, for with the Lord is unfailing love all through the watches of the night. With the Lord is *full* redemption. He does not just forgive some of your sins or solve part of your problem. He himself will redeem Israel—and that includes us Gentiles who trust Israel's Messiah—from all their sins.

Of the varied images of salvation in the Bible, redemption speaks most vividly of freedom from the slave market of sin. You and I are enslaved by our sins, but then the Redeemer comes along and purchases us and sets us free. No more slavery to sin.

On a summer day in 1830, all the slaves in the British West

Indies were to be set free. The long labor of Wilberforce and others for emancipation was at last completed, and on August 1st, these slaves would no longer be chattel or property; they'd be men. On the night before freedom day, tens of thousands of slaves never went to bed. They met in places of worship, they read God's Word, they prayed and sang and waited for the morning. They even sent watchmen up into the mountains to see the sun come up over the horizon and send word to the villages below, "We're free!"

That morning will come. So wait for the morning. Wait for the morning.

Amen.

Select Bibliography

Achtemeier, Elizabeth. *Nature, God, and Pulpit.* Eerdmans, 1992.

Achtemeier, Elizabeth. "Preaching from the Psalms." *Review and Expositor* 81, no. 3 (Summer 1994): 437–450.

Adams, James E. *War Psalms of the Prince of Peace.* Presbyterian & Reformed, 1991.

Adams, Jay E. *Sense Appeal in the Sermons of Charles Haddon Spurgeon: Studies in Preaching, Volume 1.* Presbyterian and Reformed, 1976.

Alden, Robert L. "Chiastic Psalms: A Study in the Mechanics of Semitic Poetry." *Journal of the Evangelical Theological Society* 17, no. 1 (Winter, 1974): 11–28.

Allen, Ronald J. *Contemporary Biblical Interpretation for Preachers.* Judson, 1984.

Allen, Ronald J. "Shaping Sermons by the Language of the Text." Pages 29–59 in *Preaching Biblically.* Edited by Don M. Wardlaw. Westminster, 1983.

Allender, Dan B., and Tremper Longman. *Cry of the Soul: How Our Emotions Reveal Our Deepest Questions About God.* NavPress, 1994.

Alter, Robert. *The Art of Biblical Poetry.* Basic Books, 1985.

Alter, Robert. *The Art of Biblical Literature.* Basic Books, 1992.

Anderson, Bernhard. *Out of the Depths.* Westminster, 1983.

Arnold, Carroll C. *Criticism of Oral Rhetoric.* Charles E. Merrill, 1974.

Arthurs, Jeffrey D. *Preaching with Variety: How to Re-create the Dynamics of Biblical Genres.* Kregel, 2007.

Arthurs, Jeffrey D. *Devote Yourself to the Public Reading of Scripture.* Kregel, 2012.

Attridge, Harold W., and Margot Fassler, eds. *Psalms in Community.* Society of Biblical Literature, 2003.

Bartow, Charles. *Effective Speech Communication in Leading Worship.* Abingdon, 1998.

Bland, Dave, and David Fleer, eds. *Performing the Psalms.* Chalice, 2005.

Bonhoeffer, Dietrich. *Psalms: The Prayer Book of the Bible.* Augsburg, 1974.

Bosma, Carl J. "Discerning the Voices in the Psalms: A Discussion of Two Problems in Psalmic Interpretation, Part 2." *Calvin Theological Journal* 44 (2009): 127–170.

Brueggemann, Walter. *The Prophetic Imagination.* Fortress, 1978.

Brueggemann, Walter. "The Prophet as a Destabilizing Presence." Pages 51–52 in *The Pastor as Prophet.* Edited by Earl E. Shelp and Ronald H. Sunderland. The Pilgrim Press, 1985.

Brueggemann, Walter. "Preaching as Reimagination." *Theology Today* 52, no. 3 (October 1995): 313–329.

Brueggemann, Walter. "Psalms in Narrative Performance." Pages 9–29 in *Performing the Psalms*. Edited by Dave Bland and David Fleer. Chalice, 2005.

Calvin, John. *Commentary on the Book of Psalms*. Translated by James Anderson. Eerdmans, 1998.

Ciardi, John. *How Does a Poem Mean?* 2nd ed. Houghton Mifflin, 1975.

Corbett, Edward P.J. *Classical Rhetoric for the Modern Student*. 3rd ed. Oxford University Press, 1990.

Cox, James W., ed. *Biblical Preaching*. Westminster, 1983.

Craddock, Fred. *As One Without Authority*. 3rd ed. Abingdon, 1981.

Craddock, Fred. *Preaching*. Abingdon, 1985.

Fasol, Al. *A Guide to Self-Improvement in Sermon Delivery*. Baker, 1983.

Firth, David, and Philip S. Johnson, eds. *Interpreting the Psalms*. IVP, 2005.

Goldingay, John. *Songs from a Strange Land*. InterVarsity, 1978.

Goldingay, John. *Models for the Interpretation of Scripture*. Eerdmans, 1995.

Gowan, Donald. *Reclaiming the Old Testament for the Christian Pulpit*. John Knox, 1980.

Greidanus, Sidney. *The Modern Preacher and the Ancient Text*. InterVarsity, 1988.

Hicks, John Mark. "Preaching Imprecatory Psalms" http://johnmarkhicks.com/wp-content/uploads/sites/10/2008/04/imprecatory-psalms.doc.

Hoffmann, Manfred. *Rhetoric and Theology*. University of Toronto Press, 1994.

Jacks, G. Robert. *Getting the Word Across: Speech Communication for Pastors and Lay Leaders*. Eerdmans, 1995.

Kilby, Clyde. *Christianity and Aesthetics*. IVP, 1961.

Kooienga, William. *Elements of Style for Preaching*. Zondervan, 1989.

Kugel, James. *The Idea of Biblical Poetry*. Yale University Press, 1981.

Arthurs, Jeffrey D. *Devote Yourself to the Public Reading of Scripture*. Kregel, 2012.

Lewis, C.S. *Reflections on the Psalms*. Harcourt Brace Jovanovich, 1958.

Long, Thomas G. *Preaching and the Literary Forms of the Bible*. Fortress, 1989.

Longman, Tremper. "From Weeping to Rejoicing." Pages 219–228 in *The Psalms: Language for All Seasons of the Soul*. Edited by Andrew Schmutzer and David M. Howard. Moody, 2013.

Lowry, Eugene. *How to Preach a Parable*. Abingdon, 1989.

Lowry, Eugene. "The Revolution of Sermonic Shape." Pages 93–112 in *Listening to the Word: Studies in Honor of Fred B. Craddock*. Edited by Gail O'Day and Thomas G. Long. Abingdon, 1993.

Macleod, Donald. "Preaching from the Psalms." Pages 102–118 in *Biblical Preaching*. Edited by James W. Cox. Westminster, 1983.

Mays, James L. *Preaching and Teaching the Psalms*. Westminster John Knox, 2006.

McCann, J. Clinton, Jr. *A Theological Introduction to the Book of Psalms*. Abingdon, 1993.

McCann, J. Clinton, and James C. Howell. *Preaching the Psalms*. Abingdon, 2001.

McComiskey, Thomas. *Reading Scripture in Public*. Baker, 1991.

McCutchan, Stephen P. *Experiencing the Psalms*. Smyth & Helwys, 2000.

Miller, Patrick. *Interpreting the Psalms*. Fortress, 1986.

Mitchell, Henry. *Celebration and Experience in Preaching*. Abingdon, 1990.

Nichols, Sue. *Words on Target*. John Knox Press, 1963.

O'Day, Gail, and Thomas G. Long, eds. *Listening to the Word*. Abingdon, 1993.

Perrine, Laurence. *Sound and Sense: An Introduction to Poetry*. 6th ed. Harcourt, Brace, Jovanovich, 1973.

Preminger, Alex, and Edward L. Greenstein, eds., *The Hebrew Bible in Literary Criticism* (Ungar, 1986), 286.

Raabe, Paul R. "Deliberate Ambiguity in the Psalter." *Journal of Biblical Literature* 110 (1991): 213–227.

Rang, Jack. *How to Read the Bible Aloud*. Paulist, 1994.

Ryken, Leland. *Triumph of the Imagination*. InterVaristy, 1979.

Ryken, Leland. "Metaphor in the Psalms." *Christianity and Literature* 21, no. 3 (Spring, 1982): 22–23

Ryken, Leland. *Words of Delight*. Baker, 1992.

Ryken, Leland, James C. Wilhoit, and Tremper Longman III, eds. *Dictionary of Biblical Imagery*. InterVarsity, 1998.

Schökel, Luis Alonso, and Adrian Graffy. *A Manual of Hebrew Poetics*. Gregorian Biblical Press, 1988.

Spurgeon, Charles Haddon. *C.H. Spurgeon's Sermons on the Psalms*. Vol. 9 of *Library of Spurgeon's Sermons*. Edited by Charles T. Cook. Zondervan, 1960.

Stevenson, Dwight. *In the Biblical Preacher's Workshop*. Abingdon, 1967.

Stevenson, Dwight, and Charles F. Diehl. *Reaching People from the Pulpit*. Baker, 1958.

Troeger, Thomas. *Rage, Reflect, Rejoice*. Westminster, 1977.

Troeger, Thomas. *Creating Fresh Images for Preaching*. Judson, 1982.

Wardlaw, Don M., ed. *Preaching Biblically*. Westminster, 1983.

Wiersbe, Warren. *Preaching and Teaching with Imagination*. Victor, 1994.

Wenham, Gordon J. *Psalms as Torah*. Baker, 2012.

Whybray, Norman. *Reading the Psalms as a Book.* Sheffield Academic Press, 1996.

Wilson, Paul Scott. *The Practice of Preaching.* Abingdon, 1995.

Wilson, Paul Scott. *Imagination of the Heart.* Abingdon, 1998.

Wilson, Paul Scott. "Reading the Psalms for Preaching." Pages 102–120 in *Performing the Psalms.* Edited by Dave Bland and David Fleer. Chalice, 2005.

Subject Index

Index of Psalms Discussed

CPSIA information can be obtained
at www.ICGtesting.com
Printed in the USA
FSHW020950050521
81077FS